Object Technology

A Manager's Guide

Second Edition

David A. Taylor, Ph.D.

ADDISON-WESLEY

An Imprint of Addison Wesley Longman, Inc.

Reading, Massachusetts • Harlow, England • Menlo Park, California

Berkeley, California • Don Mills, Ontario • Sydney • Bonn • Amsterdam

Tokyo • Mexico City

The first edition of this book was published under the title *Object-Oriented Technology: A Manager's Guide.*

The publisher offers discounts on this book when ordered in quantity for special sales. For more information please contact:

Corporate, Government, and Special Sales Group
Addison-Wesley Publishing Company
One Jacob Way
Reading, Massachusetts 01867

Library of Congress Cataloging-in-Publication Data

Taylor, David A.

    Object technology : a manager's guide / David A. Taylor.—2nd ed.
      p. cm.
    ISBN 0-201-30994-7
    1. Object-oriented methods (Computer science)
    QA76.9.063T39 1997   97–35870
                                                            CIP

Executive Editor: J. Carter Shanklin
Assistant Editor: Angela Buenning
Project Manager: John Fuller
Copy Editor: Jean Peck
Proofreader: Phyllis Coyne Proofreading Service
Index: Northwind Editorial Services
Composition: NK Graphics
Cover Design: Chris Norum
Cover art: © 1980 by Jay Dunitz

Text printed on recycled and acid-free paper.
ISBN 0-201-30994-7
3 4 5 6 7 8 CRW 02 01 00 99
3rd Printing February 1999

To T. Pao Liem, for having the vision to see the future of business computing and the determination to transform that vision into reality

Contents

1.
Three Keys to Object Technology

2.
Objects: Natural Building Blocks

3.
Messages: Activating Objects

4.
Classes: Implementing Objects

5.
Objects as Software Components

6.
Storing and Sharing Objects

7.
Beyond Programs and Databases

8.
Objects for the Enterprise

9.
The Adaptive Organization

Acknowledgments

I would like to thank GemStone Systems for making this book possible not once but twice. I wrote the first edition when I worked for the company—then called Servio—and they provided me with all the time and resources I needed to make the book worthy of the wide readership it has subsequently enjoyed. Now, seven years later, they have been kind enough to turn the book over to me so that I can write this new edition. GemStone is a great company with a world-class product. Next time you're on the Web, point your browser to *www.gemstone.com* and get to know them.

I would also like to express my appreciation to the reviewers of the new edition. Because of their generous efforts, this book is truer to both its subject and its audience. My profound thanks to Charles Berezin of The Davis Group, Inc.; Jack Carter of Object Space; David Chappell of Chappell and Associates; Perry Cole of MCI; Brian Edwards of GemStone; Steve Forgey of Advex Design; Ian Gilmour of Technology Transfer; Richard Hubert of iO Software; Edgar Odenwalder of Inform Worldwide; Jack Ring of Innovation Management; Moira Seed of Gem Consulting; Steve Verba of Realty One; and, last in the alphabet but foremost in her contributions, Rebecca Wirfs-Brock of Parc Place-Digitalk.

A very heartfelt thanks goes to Michael Taylor, chief architect at Enterprise Engines. It is rare in our generation when a son follows in his father's footsteps; it is especially rewarding when he steps alongside to help blaze the trail. Mike not only has become a master Java programmer but also has developed an understanding of object technology that is deeper than my own in many places. His insights into the impact of message interfaces, in particular, have had a strong influence on my thinking and on this book.

Finally, a warm thanks to my editor, Carter Shanklin, for his efforts to make a second edition possible and for his help in having the second-generation book maintain the best qualities of the original. I have enjoyed working with the people at Addison-Wesley in both generations of this book.

Introduction

Who Should Read This Book

The purpose of this book is to introduce object-oriented technology to the broadest possible audience. The worldwide movement to object technology is proceeding at an ever-increasing pace, yet I still find that a genuine understanding of objects is the exception rather than the rule. This is unfortunate because the full benefits of objects cannot be realized if the key principles are not understood. These principles are simple, natural, and easily grasped. However, they are often masked by a seemingly impenetrable veil of jargon. This book is designed to strip away that veil by explaining objects in simple English and with graphic illustrations.

This book introduces object technology

The concern of the book is on using objects in business settings, and the focus throughout is on translating the advantages of objects into business benefits. These benefits include improving the efficiency of software development, but they go far beyond that goal. The true motivation of this book is to demonstrate how the use of object technology can help your company become an adaptive organization, able to respond rapidly to changing business conditions and outmaneuver your competition in the marketplace.

The focus is on business benefits

The book is written for managers

As the book's title suggests, the target audience is managers, not technologists. The level of manager can range all the way from project managers up through CIOs and CEOs. The common denominator that makes you a candidate for reading this book is that you want information systems that make your company more competitive. The emphasis throughout is on giving you just enough insight into objects that you can make informed decisions about this technology, without dragging you through the details of implementation.

It is also a good primer for programmers

Having declared the primary audience for the book, I should also point out that it has proven to be a good introduction for practitioners as well. One of the impediments to the effective use of object technology is that developers are often trained on object-oriented tools without first being given a proper framework for understanding what they will be doing with these tools. More than one reader of the first edition has told me that everyone seeking to become an object-oriented developer should read this book before plunging into the technology. I take that as high praise indeed, and I pass it on in case you are a technologist wondering whether this book would be of value to you.

You don't need a technical background

You don't need a technical background in order to read and learn from this book. I assume that you are generally familiar with computers and how they are used in business, but I don't assume any knowledge of software development or data management technology. If you have a good grasp of these areas, you should dive right into Chapter 1. If you don't, you should start out with the software construction primer in the appendix. Even if you are already familiar with these topics, I encourage you to quickly scan this primer just to make sure that you understand what I have in mind when I contrast the object approach with conventional software construction.

How to Read the Book

I assume you are busy, so I've tried to make it easy for you to consume this book quickly. I've kept it brief; the margins contain a "fast track" summary of every paragraph; and there are illustrations to convey key concepts in graphical form. If you want rapid access to the core ideas, just read the fast track, look over the illustrations, and dip into the text only when you want more information. The fast track and graphics make it easy to return later to pick up additional information as you need it.

The book is designed for fast access

The book is also designed to be read selectively. If all you want is the big picture, just read Chapters 1 and 9 (the "bookends"). If you prefer to read the chapters in a different sequence, I strongly suggest that you read Chapter 1 before you strike out on your own. Here is a quick overview of how the book is structured:

You can read selected chapters

- ❑ Chapter 1 stands alone as an executive summary of what objects are and how they can help you.
- ❑ Chapters 2–4 explore the inner workings of objects, providing enough detail so that you can better appreciate the power of this technology.
- ❑ Chapters 5–8 explain how objects can be scaled up from simple software components to enterprisewide business systems.
- ❑ Chapter 9 explains how you can use object technology to make your company a more adaptive, competitive organization.

To help ease the problem of jargon mentioned earlier, I have limited the use of specialized terms to those that have relevance to a business person or that are particularly useful in communicating with technical personnel. As an aid to mastering these terms, I have used **boldface type** to introduce them, and I have provided nontechnical definitions for them in a glossary at the back of the book.

There is a glossary to help with terminology

The suggested readings will take you further

If you are still hungry after you've digested the material in this book, turn to the suggested readings at the back of the book for ideas on where to go next. You will find some of the books that have influenced me over the years and helped to shape the present book.

What's New in This Edition

Much has changed in seven years

If you have already read the first edition of this book, you should read this revision to bring your knowledge up to date. So much has changed in just a few years! When I wrote the first edition, object technology was the new kid on the block struggling for recognition. Seven years later, it is a required practice in many of the world's organizations, and it appears to be the emerging standard for Internet programming. For all my optimism about objects in the first edition, even my own expectations have been exceeded!

Some promises remain unfulfilled

At the same time, object technology has failed to deliver on some of its most exciting promises. The much anticipated market for pluggable business objects has yet to materialize, and most companies are still grinding out applications line by line rather than assembling software from prebuilt components.

Object technology is still evolving

This new edition takes a hard look at both the strengths and the weaknesses of object technology. On the whole, I think the potential for objects is greater than ever. But the industry is gradually changing the way it thinks about, packages, and promotes objects, and these changes are essential if we are to fully realize the potential of the technology. As I project our progress from the past ten years into the near-term future, I predict that the next five years will see objects as the enabling technology to a new generation of adaptive business systems. This book will show how you can achieve this goal even sooner within your own organization.

When Addison-Wesley first approached me to write a new edition, I imagined that I could get away with minor revisions. How wrong I was! Although I have retained a fair amount of the original material in the early chapters, the majority of the content is new. Here is a quick preview of the new topics covered in this edition:

❑ The strategic value of objects has shifted. The theme of the first edition was increasing software productivity through the use of objects. The theme of this new book is designing adaptive business systems that allow you to quickly change your business without building new applications.

This revision is a major rewrite

Adaptivity replaces productivity

❑ Java has burst onto the scene, offering us an elegant new object language and a new standard in platform independence.

Java has arrived

❑ Partly in response to Java's robust interface mechanisms, the industry is accelerating its use of message interfaces as the primary means of linking objects together. Simple in theory, message interfaces are powerful in practice and will greatly facilitate the emergence of pluggable business components.

Interfaces simplify construction

❑ Databases for objects have gone far beyond their early beginnings and now offer the scalability and robustness necessary for mission-critical applications. The relevant question now is not whether to adopt object databases but how to integrate them with your existing database technologies.

Object databases are ready for prime time

❑ Object technology is finally breaking down the classic division between applications and databases. Persistent execution engines allow entire business systems to execute directly in the same environment that manages their storage, eliminating the need to "check out" objects into programs before they can execute their business logic.

Programs and databases are merging

Distributed objects
are now a reality

❑ Objects have gone distributed. No longer is it sufficient to design a good class hierarchy and then use it to develop better applications. The challenge today is to develop international business systems that are robust, fast, and flexible. Naturally, Internet-based distribution is essential for next-generation systems.

An Invitation to Interact

Please join our electronic community

It has been a source of great joy to me to meet people from all over the world who have benefited from the first edition of this book. You should find the second edition even more helpful, and I welcome your feedback on both the book and your experiences in the use of object technology. If you have a quick question or comment, feel free to contact me at *dtaylor@engines.com.* Better yet, visit *www.engines.com* and participate in our electronic forum on the use of objects in business. As long as we are headed in the same direction, let's share what we learn and enjoy one another's company along the way!

1

Three Keys to Object Technology

This chapter begins with what I view as the best possible motivation for adopting object technology—the fact that it is the enabling technology for a new generation of adaptive software systems that can make your company more competitive. The remainder of the chapter is an executive overview of the three key characteristics of object technology: objects, messages, and classes. These characteristics are described only in summary form here. The following three chapters provide a more in-depth examination of each.

Why Objects?

The chasm between conventional software development and true, object-oriented development is not easily crossed. A company really has to want to be on the other side in order to make the leap successfully. So, it's only fair to begin with the most basic question: Why bother? The answer, in a nutshell, is this: *Objects are the enabling technology for adaptive business systems.*

Objects support adaptive business systems

The Adaptive Organization

Natural selection, the engine of adaptation in all living systems, has just shifted into high gear. It is now operating at the level of organizations rather than organisms, and the cycle of adaptations is measured in months rather than millennia. The competitive environment of business is continuously changing, and the pace of that change is increasing at an accelerating rate. Where it was once possible for a company to stake out its marketing turf and defend its position for years, static positioning is now viable only in a few isolated industries. For most companies today, the only constant is change.

Constant change is the new reality

How is a company to cope with this kind of change? The message from the management gurus is clear and consistent: The key to survival in today's chaotic business environment is rapid adaption. The adaptive organization can move quickly into new market niches, deliver custom solutions instead of fixed products, and continuously outmaneuver its competition in the ongoing battle for market share.

Unfortunately, it's a lot easier to preach the benefits of adaptivity than to realize them. Organizations have a natural inertia that inhibits any change in direction, and that inertia increases with the mass of the company. Much of the resistance stems from human nature—people stake out their turf within organizations and tend to oppose any change that threatens their position. Reward structures keyed to quarterly earnings only serve to reinforce the status quo and discourage rapid change. But even if all the human and organizational barriers to change could be overcome, there is another source of inertia with a mass approximating that of a black hole—namely, corporate information systems.

From Productivity to Adaptivity

The software construction primer in the appendix offers a quick overview of the way we build information systems and how that approach has evolved over the past 50 years. Although information systems now allow organizations to do things that would have been unthinkable prior to the advent of computers, there is one thing they hinder far more than help: the process of change. Large information systems are notoriously resistant to change, so much so that many companies find themselves locked in place by the very systems that helped them to become competitive just a few short years ago.

For many years, the standard answer to this problem was to increase the speed of software development. Fourth-generation languages (4GLs), computer-aided software engineering (CASE) tools, and yes, object technology, have all promised and failed to deliver the "order-of-magnitude productivity improvement" that has long served as the holy grail of software development. Although I remain convinced that objects can deliver on that promise, I no longer believe it is the right goal. We have passed the point where building new applications faster can solve the problem. No matter how much we accelerate the development process, the increasing pace of business change will continue to outstrip our ability to create new software.

Faster development is not the answer

The only enduring solution to the challenge of constant change lies in the development of adaptive business systems—systems that can change at least as fast as the organizations they support. This is a radical departure from the time-honored practice of developing new applications from scratch to meet new business requirements. It requires us to construct software systems of sufficient flexibility that they can quickly be modified in response to new opportunities and challenges. In short, the answer lies not in productivity but in adaptivity.

The answer lies in adaptivity

The Enabling Technology

The key benefit of object technology is that it is the enabling technology for adaptive business systems. However, this adaptivity is not an automatic consequence of adopting objects. Many companies are using objects simply as a different tool for doing what they have always done—creating new applications to solve specific business problems. Objects themselves are naturally adaptive units of software, but they lose all their flexibility if they are locked into conventional applications.

Object technology enables adaptivity

Adaptivity can be scaled to the enterprise

The key to building adaptive systems is to understand and uphold the principles of object technology at every level of a system, from the lowest-level object to the enterprise itself. Fortunately, this isn't very hard to do. The most difficult part is simply getting out of the way—setting aside our preconceptions of how software should be built and discovering where objects will take us if we remain true to their principles as we build our way up to the enterprise.

This book offers a path to that future

The purpose of this book is twofold: to provide a firm grounding in the principles of object technology and to explore the future of adaptive systems that objects make possible. This chapter provides an executive summary of the principles to make them as accessible as possible. Later chapters deepen your understanding of these principles and then begin the process of scaling objects up to the enterprise.

The Three Keys

Three features define object technology

The definition of **object technology** has been a source of debate throughout its history. However, there *is* an industry-standard definition of object-oriented technology, and it can be summarized in terms of three key concepts:

1. Objects that provide encapsulation of procedures and data
2. Messages that support polymorphism across objects
3. Classes that implement inheritance within class hierarchies

These three concepts and their associated terminology are explained in the remaining sections of this chapter. But even without further explanation, the three concepts can be used to make a distinction between languages that are and are not object-oriented. There are many object-oriented languages on the market today. Identifying a few may help you put the discussion of basic principles in a commercial context.

Many object languages are available

The object languages that are most widely used in commercial applications are **Smalltalk**, **C++**, and **Java**. Eiffel has gained widespread acceptance in Europe; the latest version of Ada qualifies as object-oriented; and Object COBOL is finally making its way into the market. Of all the object languages currently available, Java is having the greatest impact on the industry and shows the most promise for building adaptive business systems.

Examples include Smalltalk, C++, and Java

By contrast, the original versions of C, Ada, and COBOL are anything but object-oriented. Closer to the border are languages like Visual Basic (VB), which began as a conventional language but now supports most of the mechanisms of object technology. As you can see from the examples, many languages are adding object features, so the list of options is constantly growing. Visual Basic is a good illustration of this—all that version 5 lacks is inheritance, and VB could very well be fully object-oriented in its next release. The important point is not whether a language is "truly" object-oriented but how easy it is to apply the principles of objects in the environment provided by the language.

Counterexamples include Visual Basic

Objects and Encapsulation

Simula was the first object language

Although object technology came into the commercial limelight relatively recently, it's actually more than 25 years old. All the basic concepts of the object approach were introduced in the Simula programming language developed in Norway during the late 1960s.

Modeling Physical Objects

Simula was built to simulate real-world processes

Simula, an acronym for "simulation language," was created to support computer simulations of real-world processes. The authors of Simula, O. J. Dahl and Kristen Nygaard, wanted to build accurate working models of complex physical systems that could contain many thousands of components.

In Simula, modules are based on physical objects

It was apparent even back in the 1960s that modular programming is essential for building complex systems, and modularization played a central role in the design of Simula. What is special about Simula is the way in which modules are defined. They are not based on procedures, as they are in conventional programming. In Simula, modules are based on the physical objects being modeled in the simulation.

This is a natural way to define modules

This choice makes a lot of sense because the objects in a simulation offer a very natural way of breaking down the problem to be solved. Each object has a range of behavior to be modeled, and each has to maintain some information about its own status. The interaction of these objects defines the simulation. Why look for some other way to package procedures and data when the real world has already organized them for you?

Inside Objects

The concept of software objects arose out of the need to model real-world objects in computer simulations. An **object** is a software package that contains a collection of related procedures and data. These procedures are often called **methods** to distinguish them from conventional procedures that aren't attached to objects. In keeping with traditional programming terminology, the data elements are usually referred to as **variables** because their values can vary over time. The following illustration shows how methods and variables fit together to form an object.

Software objects combine procedures and data

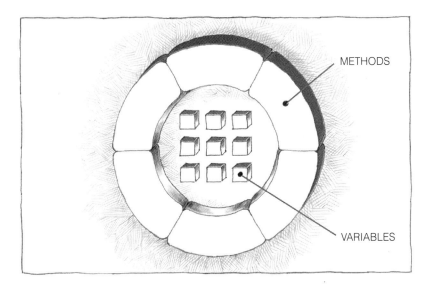

METHODS

VARIABLES

An object

For example, consider how you might represent an automated guided vehicle (AGV) in the simulation of a factory. The vehicle can exhibit a variety of behaviors, such as moving from one location to another or loading and unloading its contents. It must also maintain information about its characteristics (pallet size, lifting capacity, maximum speed, and so on) as well as its current state (contents, location, orientation, and velocity).

Example: modeling an automated vehicle

To represent the vehicle as an object, you would program its behaviors as methods and declare variables to contain information about its characteristics and states. During the simulation, the object would carry out its various methods, changing its variables as needed to reflect the effects of its actions.

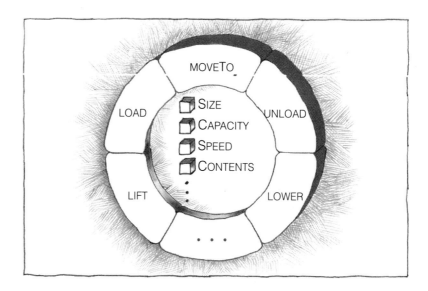

The concept of an object is simple yet powerful. Objects make ideal software modules because they can be defined and maintained independently of one another, with each object forming a neat, self-contained universe. Everything an object "knows" is captured in its variables, and everything it can do is expressed in its methods.

Messages and Polymorphism

Sending a Message

Real-world objects can exhibit an infinite variety of effects on one another—creating, destroying, lifting, attaching, buying, bending, sending, and so on. This tremendous variety raises an interesting problem: How can all these different kinds of interactions be represented in software?

Objects can interact in a rich variety of ways

The authors of Simula came up with an elegant solution to this problem: the message. The way objects interact with one another is to send messages asking objects to carry out their methods. A **message** is simply the name of an object followed by the name of a method the object knows how to execute. If a method requires any additional information in order to know precisely what to do, the message includes that information as a collection of data elements called **parameters**. The object that initiates a message is called the **sender** of that message, and the object that receives the message is called the **receiver**.

Interactions are expressed as messages

To make an automated vehicle move to a new location, for example, some other object might send it the following message:

Example: moving an automated vehicle

> *vehicle104 moveTo: binB7*

In this example, *vehicle104* is the name of the receiver, *moveTo* is the method it is being asked to execute, and *binB7* is a parameter telling the receiver where to go.

Message to _vehicle104_

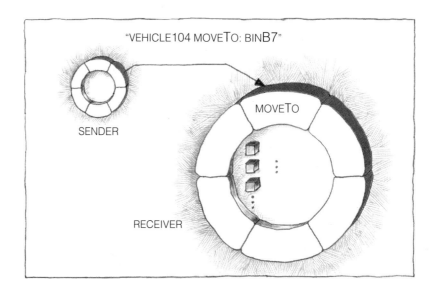

"VEHICLE104 MOVETO: BINB7"

SENDER

MOVETO

RECEIVER

Communication relies on message signatures

In order for a message to make sense, the sender and receiver must agree on the format of the message. This format is stipulated in a **message signature** that specifies the name of the method to be executed and the parameters to be included. The *moveTo* message in the present example has a simple signature: Its name is *moveTo*, and it sends one parameter, which must be a location. The signature requires all senders of this message to identify it by that name and to supply exactly one parameter of the correct type. In the context of object interactions, the shorter term **signature** is often used.

Messages support all possible interactions

An object program, then, consists of a number of objects interacting by sending messages to one another. Since everything an object can do is expressed by its methods, this simple mechanism supports all possible interactions between objects.

Responding to a Message

The fact that methods are always associated with specific objects has an interesting side effect that turns out to be highly advantageous. Different objects can respond to the same generic message, but each object can interpret the message in a different way. For example, a truck object could implement its own version of the *moveTo* message, as could a ship, a train, an aircraft, a person, or anything else that moves. The way these real-world objects determine their routes, plan their movements, and carry out these movements differs radically. But all of them would understand a common request to go to a specified destination.

Many objects can implement one message

The ability of different objects to respond to the same message in different ways is called **polymorphism**, a Greek term meaning "many forms." The term can be intimidating, and polymorphism is often considered an advanced concept in object technology. But the basic idea couldn't be simpler: Each object can have a unique response to the same message.

This feature is called polymorphism

For most business people, polymorphism is so obvious that they have a hard time seeing what is so special about it. The reason is that human communication is naturally polymorphic. You can ask a dozen people the same question and they could all determine their answers in a different way, but the meaning of the question and the form of the answer would be the same across all of them. You don't much care about their private mental processes; you just want to hear their answers. All polymorphism does is allow object interactions to enjoy some of the same flexibility as human interactions.

Human communication is polymorphic

*Polymorphism is a
great simplifier*

The real surprise to most business people is that software doesn't normally work this way. In conventional programming, procedures aren't attached to objects, and every name must be unique. This means that you would have to call a different procedure for each kind of object in order to get it to do something different. The simple *moveTo* message would turn into an open-ended list of specialized requests: *AGVMoveTo, truckMoveTo, shipMoveTo, trainMoveTo, aircraftMoveTo, personMoveTo,* and so on. It seems like a rather cumbersome way to build software in retrospect, but there was no other way to do it prior to objects.

Classes and Inheritance

*There may be many
objects of a given
kind*

Sometimes, a simulation involves only a single example of a particular kind of object. It is much more common, however, to need more than one object of each kind. An automated factory, for example, might have any number of guided vehicles. This possibility raises another concern: It would be extremely inefficient to redefine the same methods in every single occurrence of that object.

Templates for Objects

*Classes define groups
of similar objects*

Here again, the authors of Simula came up with an elegant solution: the class. A **class** is a software template that defines the methods and variables to be included in a particular kind of object. The methods and variables that make up the object are defined only once, in the definition of the class. The objects that belong to a class—commonly called **instances** of that class—contain only their own particular values for the variables.

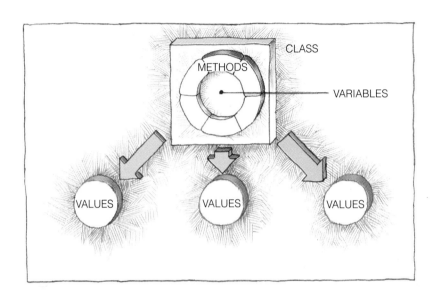

To continue the previous example, a simulated factory might contain many automated vehicles, each of which carried out the same actions and maintained the same kinds of information. All such vehicles would be represented by a class called *AutomatedVehicle*, which would define its methods and variables. The actual vehicles would be represented by instances of this class, each with its own unique identity (*vehicle101*, *vehicle102*, *vehicle103*, and so on). Each of these instances would contain data values that represented its own particular contents and location.

Example: the automated vehicle class

Another important function of classes is to specify the messages that objects of this kind will make available to other objects. The set of messages an object commits to respond to is called its **message interface**. This interface is specified as a collection of message signatures, each of which defines the name and parameters for a particular message. The only design requirement placed on a class is that it provide a method to implement each message specified in its interface. The internals of the class are completely hidden be-

Classes also define message interfaces

hind this interface and may include any number of variables as well as "invisible" methods that are used only by the object itself.

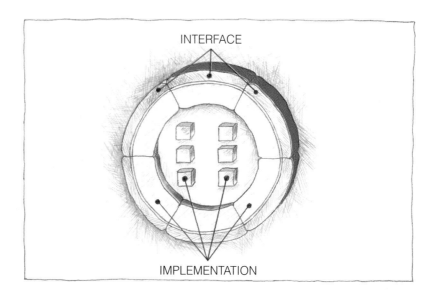

INTERFACE

IMPLEMENTATION

*Objects are instances
of classes*

An object, then, is an instance of a particular class. Its methods and variables are defined in the class, and its values are stored in the instance. To keep my explanations simple, I usually talk about objects wherever possible, referring to classes and instances only when it's important to point out where the object's information is actually stored. For example, if I say that the object *vehicle104* has a method called *moveTo*, this is simply a more convenient way of saying that *vehicle104* is an instance of a class that defines a method called *moveTo*.

Inheriting Class Information

Simula took the concept of classes one step further by allowing classes to be defined as special cases of each other. If you needed to represent two different kinds of automated vehicle, you could define one vehicle class in detail and then define the other as everything in the first class plus any additional methods and variables you wanted to add. Simply by declaring the second class to be a special case of the first, you would automatically give it access to everything the first class could do.

Classes can be defined in terms of each other

The mechanism whereby one class of objects can be defined as a special case of a more general class is known as **inheritance**. Special cases of a class are commonly known as **subclasses** of that class; the more general class, in turn, is known as the **superclass** of its special cases. In addition to the methods and variables they inherit, subclasses may define their own methods and variables. They can also redefine any of the inherited methods, a technique known as **overriding**.

Inheritance is the mechanism that allows this

Subclasses of a super-class

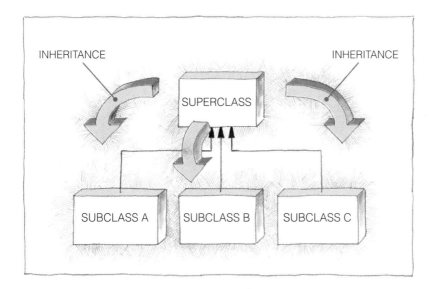

For example, the class *AutomatedVehicle* could be broken down into two subclasses, *PalletAGV* and *RollAGV*, each of which inherited the general characteristics of the parent class. Either subclass could establish its own special characteristics by adding to the parent's definition or by overriding its behavior.

Two subclasses of automated vehicle

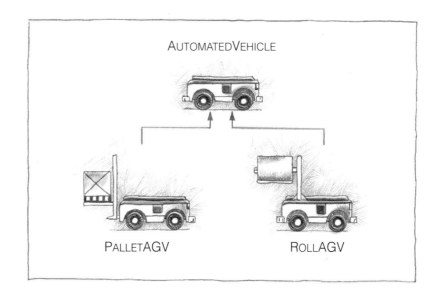

AUTOMATEDVEHICLE

PALLETAGV   **ROLLAGV**

Message interfaces
are also inherited

Because classes define message interfaces, these interfaces are also inherited by their subclasses. This means that all the subclasses of a given class are guaranteed to respond to any messages that can be handled by the parent class. This is an extremely useful property because it allows us to treat all the specialized forms of a class as equivalent at the general level.

Example: an unlim-
ited variety of prod-
ucts

For example, if we define a *Product* class that includes messages for production, pricing, and shipping in its interface, then we have an ironclad guarantee that all the subclasses of *Product* will implement all these messages. Any given subclass may use the implementations it inherits from *Product*, or it may define its own implementations; it doesn't matter to us at this level. What matters is that we can design our system to produce, price, and ship an unlimited variety of products without having to be concerned about how each specialized type carries out these tasks.

Hierarchies of Classes

Classes can be nested to any degree, and inheritance will automatically accumulate down through all the levels. The resulting treelike structure is known as a **class hierarchy**. A class called *Part*, for example, could be broken down into special kinds of parts such as *Motor, Chassis, Connector,* and so on. *Motor*, in turn, could be divided into *DriveMotor* and *SteppingMotor*, each of which could be broken down further as needed. An instance of, say, *VariableSpeedDriveMotor* would inherit all the characteristics of the *Part* class, as well as those of *Motor* and *DriveMotor*.

Hierarchies of classes can be built up

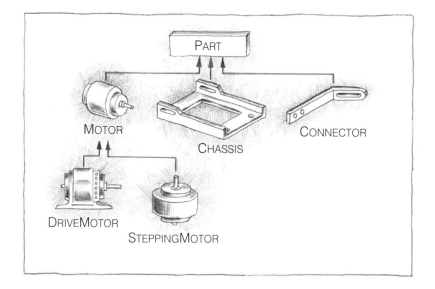

A class hierarchy for parts

*Class hierarchies re-
flect human under-
standing*

Class hierarchies increase the ability of objects to reflect the way we view the real world. Human knowledge is often organized in a hierarchical manner, relying on generic concepts and their refinement into increasingly specialized cases. Object technology takes the same conceptual mechanisms we employ in everyday life and uses them to build sophisticated yet understandable software systems. This is particularly evident in the generalization and specialization provided by a class hierarchy.

2

Objects: Natural Building Blocks

Object programming is often said to be more natural than traditional programming, and this is true on a couple of different levels. On one level, object programming is more natural because it allows us to organize information in ways that are familiar to us, as illustrated in the class hierarchies described in the preceding chapter. On a deeper level, it is more natural in that it reflects nature's own techniques for managing complexity. This chapter opens and closes with brief looks at the structure of living organisms to establish a framework for understanding the adaptive nature of objects. The remainder of the chapter looks at the actual technology underlying objects and demonstrates why objects provide a better foundation for flexible business systems.

Nature's Building Blocks

The basic building block out of which all living things are composed is the cell. Cells are organic "packages" that, like objects, combine related information and behavior. Most of the information is contained in protein molecules within the nucleus of the cell. The behavior, which may range from energy conversion to movement, is carried out by structures outside the nucleus.

Cells encapsulate data and behavior

Cells are surrounded by a membrane that permits only certain kinds of chemical exchanges with other cells. This membrane protects the internal workings of the cell from outside intrusion, and it also hides the complexity of the cell and presents a relatively simple interface to the rest of the organism. All interactions between cells take place through chemical messages recognized by the cell membrane and passed through to the inside of the cell.

Cells communicate through messages

A living cell

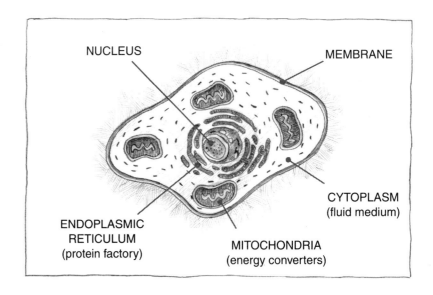

This message-based communication greatly simplifies the way cells function. The cells don't have to read each others' protein molecules or control each others' structures to get what they need from each other. All they do is send the appropriate chemical message, and the receiving cell responds accordingly.

This simplifies the interactions between cells

The cell is truly a universal building block. All cells share a common structure and operate according to the same basic principles. Within this generic structure, however, infinite variability is possible. For example, plant cells have a hard outer wall to make them rigid; blood cells are mobile and specialized to transport gases; and muscle cells are able to distort their shape to perform mechanical work. But this tremendous variability is not chaotic; it's all neatly organized—or "classified"—in a hierarchy of specialized types and subtypes. The accompanying diagram gives the merest hint of the depth and breadth of this diversity.

Living cells are ideal building blocks

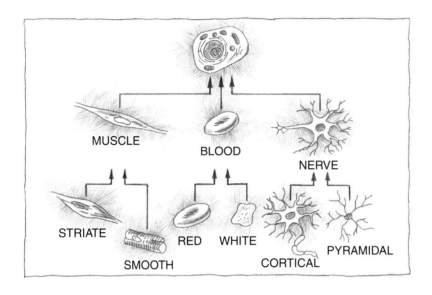

Objects, as defined in object technology, have many of the essential characteristics of living cells. A closer look inside the structure of an object reveals some of these similarities.

Objects are like cells

The Anatomy of an Object

Packaging related data and procedures together is called **encapsulation**. As you can see from the structure of a cell, encapsulation is an idea that has been around for a very long time. The fact that it has worked so well in natural systems suggests that we may be on the right track with this mechanism!

Placing data with behavior is called encapsulation

Encapsulating Objects

*The message inter-
face surrounds the
object*

The key to object encapsulation is the message interface. As the accompanying illustration indicates, this interface surrounds the object and acts as the point of contact for all incoming messages. The
message interface serves the same function as the membrane of a
cell—to provide an essential barrier between the internal structure
of the object and everything that lies outside the object. Like a
cell's membrane, the message interface ensures that all interactions
with the object take place through a predefined system of messages
that the object is guaranteed to understand and handle correctly.

**Message interface sur-
rounding an object**

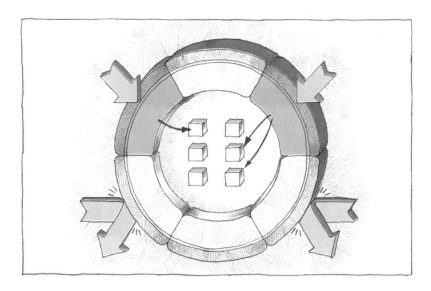

*Encapsulation pro-
motes information
hiding*

The encapsulation mechanism of object technology is a natural extension of the information-hiding strategy developed in structured
programming, as described in the software construction primer in
the appendix. Object technology improves on this strategy with
better mechanisms to pull the right kinds of information together,
including all related data and procedures, and hide their details

more effectively. There is simply no way for any other object to access the data or methods hidden behind an object's interface.

For example, data inside an object is accessed only by methods that implement the object's interface. Just as cells don't "read" each others' protein molecules, objects don't touch each others' data structures. Rather, objects send each other messages that call methods into action. These methods, in turn, access the required variables.

Data is accessed only through methods

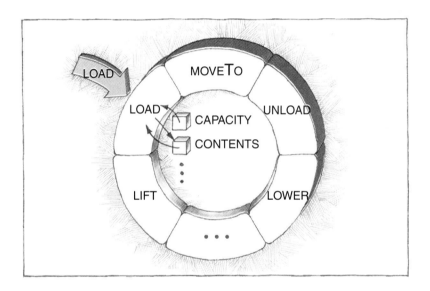

A method accessing data

This same mechanism also controls access to methods that are used only by the object itself. For example, determining the price of a product can require a complex set of interacting calculations, each of which could involve a number of methods and variables. Allowing other objects to trigger these internal methods directly could create havoc within the object. To prevent this kind of disruption, the object hides all of its pricing logic behind an interface that only allows other objects to inquire about its current price or set a new base price for future calculations.

Internal methods are also hidden

Interfaces protect the internals of objects	Message interfaces offer two important kinds of protection. First, they protect an object's internal components from being corrupted by other objects. If other objects had direct access to an object's variables and internal methods, eventually one of these other objects would handle a variable incorrectly or call the wrong method and damage the object. An object protects itself from this kind of error by hiding its variables and internal methods behind its message interface.
Interfaces protect other objects as well	The second and less obvious kind of protection works in the opposite direction. By hiding its variables and internal methods, an object protects other objects from depending on its internal structure. For example, they are spared having to keep track of each variable's name, the type of information it contains, the amount of space it takes up in storage, and a host of other details that would complicate all their procedures for accessing an object's variables. With encapsulation, an object only needs to know how to ask another object for information. All the details about how that information is stored are neatly tucked out of sight behind the message interface.

Facilitating Changes

Encapsulation facilitates changes	In addition to simplifying the interactions between objects, encapsulation also makes the modification of objects much easier than it would otherwise be. Hiding all the implementation details of an object inside its message interface allows the object to be modified extensively in response to changing business needs. As long as the portions of the message interface currently in use by other objects remain intact, internal modifications won't require changes to any other part of the system.

Consider making the following change to the *AutomatedVehicle* class discussed in the preceding chapter. When you first defined the class, you declared a fixed carrying capacity for the vehicle and stored it in a variable. Subsequently, you discover that you need to perform one of several different calculations to determine capacity depending on the kind of load involved. To make this change, you remove the capacity variable and define a set of internal methods for calculating capacity. Each of these methods might require one or more variables, so you add these variables as needed. Finally, you perform the switchover—you change the load method to call your new methods to verify that the vehicle can handle the load.

Example: modifying the automated vehicle

Changing the implementation of capacity

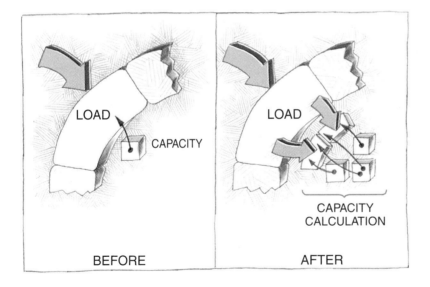

LOAD

CAPACITY

BEFORE

LOAD

CAPACITY
CALCULATION

AFTER

Change is harder in conventional systems

In a conventional system, this change would require significant restructuring. You would need to rewrite all the subroutines in the system that dealt with vehicle carrying capacities to make them call functions rather than access a data value. You would have to repeat the same selection logic for using the correct calculation in all the affected subroutines. Every routine that needed to determine capacity would have to be changed; all these changes would have to be made correctly; and all these changes would have to be synchronized to occur at the same time. Anything less would result in a broken system.

Encapsulation limits changes to a single object

In short, modeling the automated vehicle as a self-contained object allows you to restrict all your changes to a single object. There is no duplication of the selection logic, no doubt about whether all the necessary subroutines have been modified, and no synchronization problem. Just modify the *AutomatedVehicle* class, and you're done. All other objects continue to interact with it just as they did before. You have made a fundamental change in how information is handled, converting it from data to a collection of specialized procedures, and none of the other objects even "know" that a change has taken place!

Using Composite Interfaces

Interfaces may be segmented

In most cases, the message interface surrounding an object is a single, unbroken surface. However, it is possible to divide this interface into segments by first defining some simpler interfaces and then combining them into a composite interface for a particular object. This technique can be used to further protect the internals of objects by giving other objects access only to selected components of the object's overall interface.

For example, the message interface for a *Product* object might be composed of four component interfaces: one for defining the product, a second for producing it, a third for selling it, and a fourth for shipping it. Each of these interfaces deals with very different aspects of the product and would be accessed by different parts of the company, as shown in the accompanying figure.

Example: a composite Product interface

A product with four interfaces

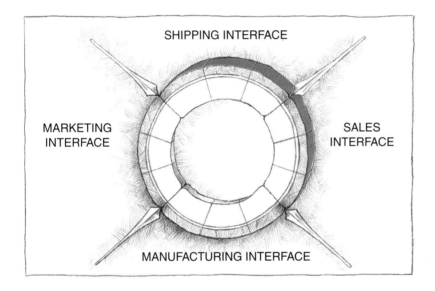

Notice that the segmentation of the message interface increases the two kinds of protection described earlier. First, other objects can't access methods they have no right to invoke. A *Sale* object, for example, couldn't get access to the manufacturing interface to change the production schedule for a product. Second, other objects are protected from changes to interfaces they don't have access to. If a change in the way a product was manufactured required changes to the interface of the *Product* object, these changes would be restricted to the manufacturing interface. Only the manufacturing object would be affected by the changes—the marketing, sales, and shipping objects would be completely unaffected.

Composite interfaces provide added protection

Constructing Composite Objects

Objects Inside Other Objects

Objects can contain other objects

The variables contained within objects can be used in two different ways. First, they can be used to store data values, such as the number 12.5 or the text string "Approved." More interestingly, they can contain references to other objects. The form of the reference is an implementation detail and varies considerably among object systems. The important point is that the reference held by a variable provides the containing object with a "handle" or effective address for the contained object, allowing the containing object to manage its component by sending it appropriate messages.

This increases their representational power

Objects that contain other objects are called **composite objects**. Composite objects are important because they can represent far more sophisticated structures than simple objects can. For example, an aircraft consists of wings, engines, and other components that are far too complex to be represented as simple numbers or text.

Components of an aircraft

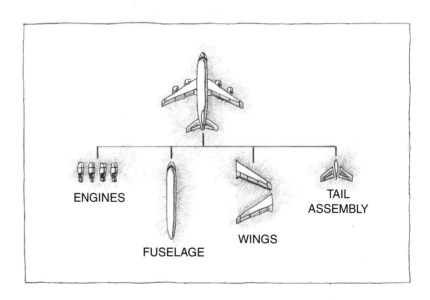

ENGINES

FUSELAGE

WINGS

TAIL ASSEMBLY

The objects contained in composite objects may themselves be composite objects, and this nesting can be carried out to any number of levels. The major components of an aircraft, for example, are very complex objects in their own right. In any reasonable model of an aircraft, each of these components would be represented by a composite object that, in all likelihood, would be composed of still more composite objects, and so on.

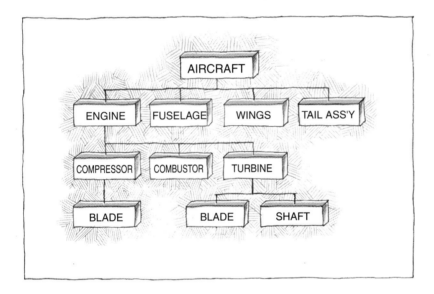

Collections of Objects

There is a special kind of class, often called the **collection class**, that can be found in the class library shipped with most commercial languages. As the name suggests, the basic function of a collection is to gather together objects that must be managed as a group. In a model of an aircraft, for example, we wouldn't create a separate named variable for every seat object. Rather, we would gather all the seat objects into a collection and place a reference to that collection in a single variable called *Seats*.

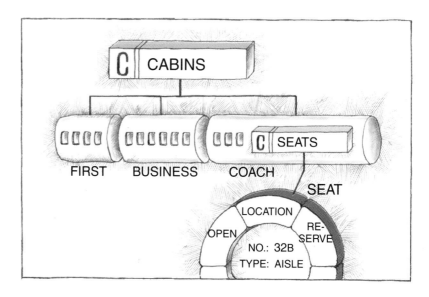

*Collections increase
flexibility*

This example illustrates how collections can simplify composite objects while also making them more flexible. In addition to reducing several hundred variables down to one, the *Seats* collection allows us to vary the number of seats without reprogramming the model. In addition, the collection makes it easier to carry out group operations on the seats, such as scanning them to see which ones are currently reserved. The method that performed this task would repeatedly ask the collection for its next element until the collection reported that it was empty. This is much simpler than writing a method to examine several hundred named variables.

The Benefits of Composition

*Composition helps
manage complexity*

Because objects can be composed of other objects, object languages can represent real-world objects at the level we naturally think about them. Even a complex, deeply nested structure such as a jet aircraft can be treated as a single, unified object. And since that complex object can have its own behavior, other objects can use it with very little awareness of its internal complexity. This is a good example of how object technology can bring order to large-scale systems. Composite objects not only keep simple things simple, they can make complex things simple as well.

Composite objects offer another important advantage—they lay the foundation for a mechanism called **delegation**, in which an object assigns a task to another object. Delegation is a very common pattern in object designs because it supports the division of labor encouraged by objects. For example, determining the charge for a telephone call is a fairly complex process because the charge can be based on physical distance, arbitrary zones, or other factors. Rather than building this complexity directly into a *Call* object, we could give *Call* a component *Rater* to perform this task. Then, the *Call* could simply send its end points and duration to the *Rater* and get back the appropriate charge. Because it would not know anything about how the *Rater* did its work, any kind of *Rater* could be placed in the *Call* without affecting the behavior of the *Call* object in any way.

Composite objects permit delegation

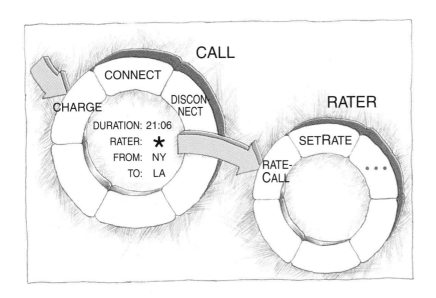

A *Call* delegating to a *Rater* object

Designing Multilevel Systems

Cells and objects have much in common

Although the actual mechanics of cells and objects could hardly be more different, their overall functions are remarkably similar. Both cells and objects encapsulate associated data and behavior; both have interfaces that define what signals they will respond to in their environment; both use message-based communication to hide complexity; both can be organized into a hierarchy of specialized types; and both provide the fundamental building blocks for constructing an infinite variety of complex systems.

This correspondence is revealing

This similarity is encouraging—the incredible variation among living organisms clearly demonstrates the flexibility of this basic approach to constructing complex systems. Moreover, pursuing the analogy could lead to important insights into the problems of software construction. Nature, after all, has been using the approach a few billion years longer than software developers have!

Living systems have multiple levels

Here is a case in point. The cell is only the most basic level of modularization in complex organisms. The next higher level is that of the organs, such as the heart and lungs. These organs, in turn, are "organized" into systems, such as the circulatory and respiratory systems. Finally, these systems combine to form the organism itself. What is fascinating about these levels of modularity is that the functioning of each level is independent of the ones below it. Replace the heart with a mechanical pump and the circulatory system continues to work quite nicely, despite the fact that the pump has a very different design and is made of radically different materials.

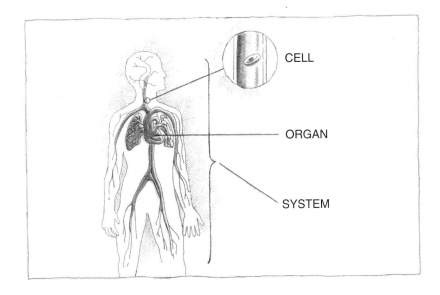

CELL

ORGAN

SYSTEM

What is particularly striking to me is how few layers are required to account for the wondrous variety and complexity of living systems. We can surely benefit from looking at the incredible results of this elegant system of multilevel modularity. If we can keep the layers independent of one another, we can build extremely sophisticated, flexible business systems with no more than three or four layers.

Software systems need these same levels

We already have the mechanism for creating these layers—the composite object. What we need to do is use this mechanism in a way that mimics the architecture of living systems. Instead of building haphazard composite objects that vary in depth and complexity, we should strive to define distinct layers of composition. Each of these layers should be a complete, understandable design in its own right, independent of both the structure of the lower levels and its uses in higher levels.

Composite objects make this possible

With such an approach, we can begin to achieve some of the robustness and adaptivity of living systems in our organizational systems. Each component will be free to evolve into better forms on its own level without disturbing the other levels, provided only that it continues to perform its functions at least as well as it has in the past. Even radical surgery should be possible with this kind of design. Imagine being able to pull the "heart" out of a business system, replace it with a component of a completely different design, and never miss a beat in the rhythm of the business!

3

Messages: Activating Objects

However carefully crafted, an object is useless in isolation. Its value comes from its interactions with other objects, and all interactions between objects take place through messages. This chapter explains what messages are and how they work. Once this foundation has been laid, techniques will be explored for making messages as flexible as possible while ensuring that they are always sent and received correctly. The final section explains how messages can be used to remove much of the complexity of business systems and allow them to be changed more readily.

The Anatomy of a Message

Components of a Message

A message consists of three parts:

1. A receiver object
2. A method the receiver knows how to execute
3. An ordered set of parameters that this method requires to carry out its function

The third part is optional; if the method doesn't need any additional information to do its job, there are no parameters.

A message has three parts

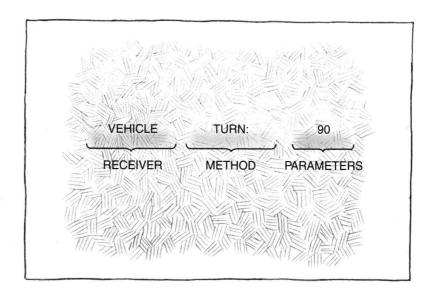

Parameters are like variables

Parameters are like variables in that they hold information that can vary from one sending of a message to another. Like variables, they may be either basic data types, such as numbers or letters, or references to other objects. The similarity of parameters and variables is no coincidence—parameters exist primarily to pass values of variables from one object to another.

Message formatting varies among languages

The way a message is written varies across languages. In general, the three components of the message appear in the order described: first receiver, then method, then parameters. But the way you identify the components and separate them from one another differs. A message in Smalltalk, for example, might look like this:

vehicle104 turn: 90

The same message in C++ or Java might look like this:

vehicle104.turn(90)

In each case, *vehicle104* is the receiving object, *turn* is the method the receiver is being asked to execute, and *90* is a parameter that specifies the angle of rotation.

In the examples that follow, I use a generic format to represent messages. It's similar to Smalltalk because that format is a bit closer to English and therefore easier to read. But the format is meant only to be explanatory and should not be taken literally.

Examples in this book use a neutral format

Responses to Messages

In most object systems, messages require some sort of response from the receiver. This response is usually called the **return value**. Return values, like parameters, can be either simple data values or objects.

Messages may require a response

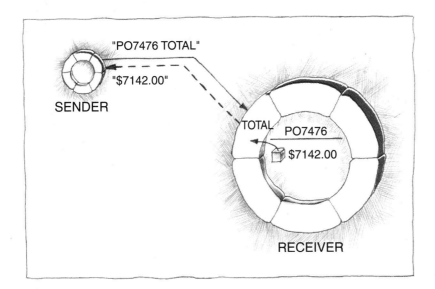

A message and its return value

"PO7476 TOTAL"

"$7142.00"

SENDER

TOTAL PO7476

$7142.00

RECEIVER

Composite objects can be returned

Only a single value can be returned by a message. This might be viewed as a limitation, but it is easily overcome. If more than one value or object must be returned, they can be packaged in a composite object. This single object is then sent back as the response to the message.

Collections return groups of objects

Collection objects are particularly useful for this purpose because they can return a variable number of objects in a single package. For example, a request for all the open seats on a particular flight could return a collection of seat objects, each of which would know its number, type, restrictions, and other characteristics.

Returning a collection of open seats

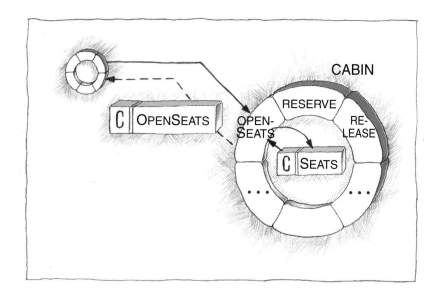

Signatures for Messages

Messages conform to signatures

In order to be understood by their receiving objects, messages must conform to assigned signatures. The signature for a message specifies the following characteristics:

Name: the name of the requested method

Parameters: the names and types of the parameters, listed in order

Notice that the identity of the receiver is not included in this list. The reason is that the signature of the message doesn't depend on who sends or receives it. All the signature does is declare the *form* of the message—it's up to the individual objects whether they can send or receive this message.

Receivers aren't part of the signature

For example, a request for open seats might have the following signature:

Example: requesting open seats

Name: *reportOpenSeatsInClass*

Parameters: *Flight*, a number

            Class, a letter

Typical values for the class parameter would be *F*, *B*, and *C*, for first, business, and coach, respectively.

Sending the Right Information

Checking Parameters

In order for a message to be correctly processed, its parameters must be of the type the receiver is expecting. Otherwise, undesirable results can occur. The message

Parameters must be of the right types

> *Warehouse ship: Liverpool to: 10,000*

won't make much sense to a *Warehouse* object if it is expecting a quantity in the first parameter and a location in the second!

Checking basic data types is easy	When basic data types are used in parameters, there is no question about how they should be checked. If the signature of a message calls for an integer number to occupy a certain parameter position, the system simply won't allow any other kind of information to be placed in this position. Because the types of all variables are determined when a system is programmed, there is no way that the wrong kind of information can appear at execution time and produce unpleasant surprises.
There are two ways to check object types	When objects are passed as parameters, there are two different options on how to check them: by their class or by their interface. The following sections explore the relative advantages of the two approaches to checking parameters.

Checking by Class

Checking by class is simple and flexible	To check a parameter by class, just enter the name of the required class as the type of the parameter. The object language will then restrict the parameter to contain only instances of that class or its subclasses. Subclasses are allowed because they are required to implement the message interface of their parent class, so they are functionally equivalent to the parent in terms of what they can do when they reach their destination. This means that a single class can be used to specify an entire family of classes for that parameter, including classes that haven't even been developed yet.
Example: shipping a product	An example will clarify how this mechanism works. Imagine that you have built an object-oriented system to help route and ship your products. When you want to make a shipment, you send a message of the following form:

ShippingDepartment ship: Product to: Customer

The constraint on the first parameter is that it be an instance of the class *Product* or one of its subclasses. It doesn't matter if you have defined a single *Product* class or a hundred, nor does it matter how deeply nested these classes are. You are also free to extend your hierarchy of *Product* classes at any time, and the new classes will automatically fit into the running system.

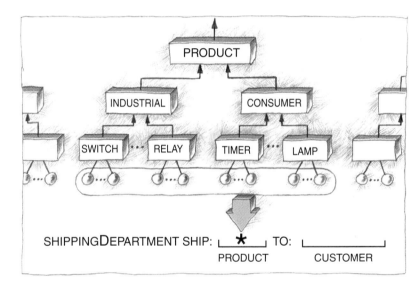

As this example illustrates, specifying parameters using classes is both efficient and flexible. To get the maximum benefit from this approach, however, you must do two things. First, you must organize your class hierarchy in a way that generic functions, such as shipping, appear at the highest level at which they are required. Second, you must specify this highest-level class as the type for a parameter.

Always specify the most generic class

Class-based checking
has limitations

Although class-based checking is simple and powerful, experience with large-scale systems has revealed some limitations. To continue the previous example, suppose that you needed to return some damaged supplies to one of your suppliers. Ideally, you would use your standard message to the shipping department:

ShippingDepartment ship: Product to: Customer

However, the supplies are not products, so the message signature won't accept the supplies object for the first parameter. Also, the vendor is not a customer, so the vendor object won't be accepted in the second parameter. In short, the message can't be used.

Checking by Interfaces

Typing by interfaces
is more flexible

The second approach to typing parameters provides the same level of safety as typing by classes while significantly increasing flexibility. To type a parameter by its interface, simply insert the interface as the type in a method signature rather than a class. Now, any object that implements this interface automatically qualifies as a parameter. The restriction to a single branch of the hierarchy is lifted.

Example: a generic
shipping message

To see this advantage, let's define a shipping message that allows anything to be shipped to any destination. The first step is to create two new interfaces: *Shipment* and *ShipmentReceiver*. The first interface contains the signatures for all the messages having to do with arranging and executing the movement of physical objects. The second interface defines the messages for scheduling incoming shipments, allocating loading docks, and the like. Now we have a perfectly generic message:

ShippingDepartment ship: Shipment to: ShipmentReceiver

Assuming that *Products* and *Supplies* both include the *Shipment* interface in their overall message interface, all *Product* and *Supply* objects, including all their subclasses, will be accepted in that parameter slot. If new kinds of objects are defined that might need to be shipped, all they have to do is implement the *Shipment* interface and they, too, can be used in the message. It doesn't matter where they are in the class hierarchy because class information is now irrelevant. The same reasoning holds for *Customers* and *Vendors*—so long as they both implement the *ShipmentReceiver* interface, they can appear as the destination in the message.

This produces a highly flexible solution

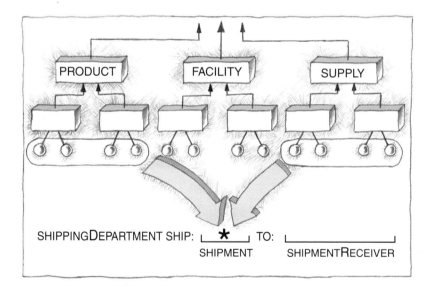

Constraining by interface

A second advantage of using interfaces to restrict parameters is that the technique allows a more precise specification of how the parameter object is supposed to interact with the receiver object. If we are sending a *Product* object to the shipping department, we don't want that department to talk to the design or sales interfaces of the *Product*. Specifying the *Shipment* interface is a clear indication that shipping should interact with the *Product* only in its capacity as something that can be transported.

Interfaces allow precise communications

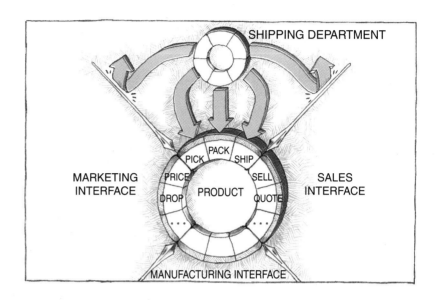

Interfaces are becoming the new types

Given that these advantages come at no cost, more and more object developers are using interfaces to define object types rather than classes. This transition is a natural evolution of object thinking. Because every class implicitly defines a message interface, the adoption of interfaces as types begins with no more than a shift in perspective.

Typing by interface is the best practice

Once designers make this mental shift, they begin to define new types by creating explicit interfaces that are not dependent on any particular class. As the added power of these independent types is experienced, they tend to use the technique with increasing frequency. The result: Message interfaces become the driving force behind object designs, and classes become vehicles for implementing these interfaces. This approach is now regarded as the best practice within the object industry.

The Power of Polymorphism

The preceding examples demonstrate **polymorphism** at work: Objects, messages, and other elements of a business system can take many different forms yet be treated equivalently within the system. This simple, self-evident mechanism makes object software more flexible, as described in Chapter 1. It also makes it much simpler.

Objects use natural communications

Simplifying Programs

Suppose we are developing a system that includes portfolios of financial instruments such as stocks and bonds. The system should allow us to perform a variety of operations on portfolios, such as adding new stocks, tracking the performance of various kinds of instruments, and monitoring the current value of the portfolio as a whole. Our first class is *Portfolio,* a composite object that contains a collection object called *FinancialInstruments.* Our first method is *add,* which takes a financial instrument object as its parameter.

Example: valuing financial instruments

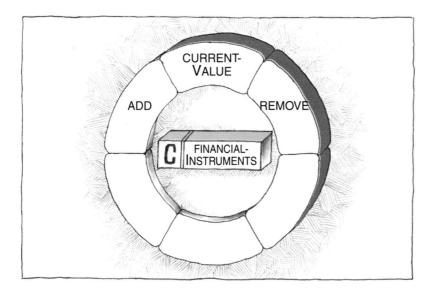

A financial portfolio

When we begin to program the method for determining the current value of the portfolio as a whole, we immediately run into a problem—there are many different kinds of financial instruments, each of which may require a different procedure for determining its current value. A stock might pull its current value from an on-line quote service, a bond would check to see whether it had reached maturity before checking its trading value, and so on. In a conventional program, each of these different procedures would require a different name—*valueStock*, *valueBond*, *valueOption*, *value-MutualFund*, and so on—so that the correct one would be invoked for each type of instrument. In order to get the current value of the portfolio, we would have to look at each instrument in turn, figure out what type it was, and then call the appropriate procedure. In simplified form, the code for a *valuePortfolio* procedure might look something like that shown in the accompanying figure.

**Choosing the right *value*
method**

```
            ⋮
  IF INSTRUMENT = STOCK THEN
       CALL VALUESTOCK
  IF INSTRUMENT = BOND THEN
       CALL VALUEBOND
  IF INSTRUMENT = OPTION THEN
       CALL VALUEOPTION
  IF INSTRUMENT = MUTUALFUND THEN
       CALL VALUEMUTUALFUND
            ⋮
```

In an object system, each kind of financial instrument would be represented by a different class. Each of these classes would include a method called *value*, and each would implement the method in the manner required by that particular financial instrument. Because each class knows only about its own version of *value*, there is no possibility of confusion within the program. Polymorphism allows the same message to be handled in different ways depending on the object that receives it.

Polymorphism solves this problem

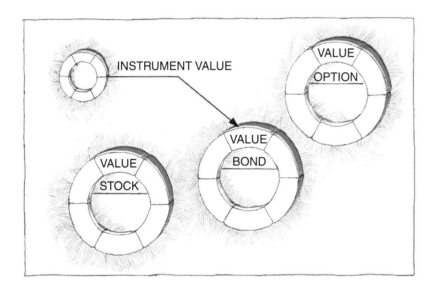

A *value* method in multiple objects

Polymorphism simplifies programs because it allows you to use the same name for the same operation everywhere in a program. It's up to the receiving object to carry out the operation in its own unique way. Polymorphism also simplifies the way in which objects request services from one another because they can use the same message for an entire family of objects. Notice how much simpler the valuation method becomes using polymorphism.

The result is simpler programs

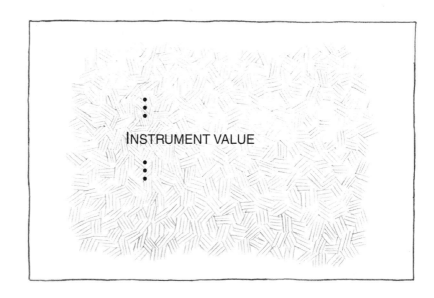

INSTRUMENT VALUE

Polymorphism reduces information load

This example is yet another illustration of the importance of information hiding. If all financial instruments use the same name for their *value* method, none of the other classes have to keep track of all the different names used for this common operation in order to send each instrument the correct message. An object can send the same message to any financial instrument in a portfolio and trust that the instrument will handle the message in the appropriate way.

Expediting Change

Conventional systems are hard to change

Polymorphism is particularly useful when you add new kinds of objects to a system. Suppose you wanted to add mortgage-backed securities to a portfolio. Using conventional techniques, you would have to trace through your system to discover all the places where financial instruments were referenced, edit each of these to incorporate the new kind of instrument, and then rebuild, retest, and redeploy the entire system. It is no wonder that it takes so long to get simple changes made to business systems!

In an object system, a new *MortgageBackedSecurity* class would implement its own *value* method. Whenever another object wanted this new instrument to value itself, the object would send it the standard *value* message, just as it does with any other financial instrument. So, all the objects that interact with financial instruments are totally unaffected by the change. You can add new financial instruments simply by adding new classes to represent them, without modifying your system in any other way.

Objects make such changes easy

To summarize, the key business benefits of polymorphism are that it makes objects more independent of one another and allows new objects to be added with minimal changes to existing objects. These benefits, in turn, lead to simpler systems that are capable of evolving gracefully over time in response to changing needs. In short, polymorphism is an essential feature of adaptive business systems.

Polymorphism is the key to adaptivity

4

Classes: Implementing Objects

Objects interacting through messages form the essence of object technology. In fact, many near-object languages support precisely these two mechanisms and use them to great advantage. But it's the concept of classes that brings order to the object approach and makes it so effective in representing complex systems. In the same way that a classification hierarchy brings order to an otherwise bewildering array of plants and animals, classes allow a company to organize its business components in a rational, understandable way. The addition of an inheritance mechanism provides further leverage by allowing methods developed for one class to be reused in other, more specialized classes, reducing development time and isolating definitions to a single point of change.

The Anatomy of a Class

The purpose of a class is to specify the behavior of its instances. This specification has two components: a message interface and an implementation of that interface. The interface specifies what the class can do, and it consists of a list of the messages the class can respond to. The implementation specifies how those responses are carried out, and it consists of method code and variable definitions. In short, the interface specifies *what* instances of a class can do, and the implementation specifies *how* they do what they do.

Classes specify interfaces and implementations

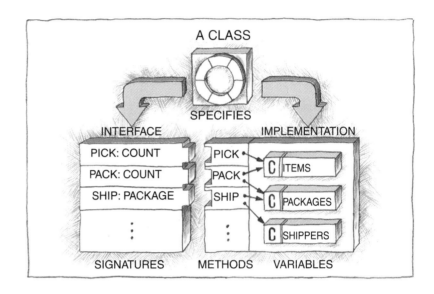

A CLASS

SPECIFIES

INTERFACE   IMPLEMENTATION

PICK: COUNT   PICK

PACK: COUNT   PACK   ITEMS

SHIP: PACKAGE   SHIP   PACKAGES

⋮   ⋮   SHIPPERS

SIGNATURES   METHODS   VARIABLES

Specifying Interfaces

*Interfaces are sets of
signatures*

A message interface is a named set of message signatures that characterize a particular kind of entity or interaction. An interface can
also contain other interfaces as components, so the grouping of signatures can become quite rich. Any class that commits to supporting a particular interface obligates itself to handle messages that
conform to the signatures contained in that interface, including
any signatures that may be contained in its component interfaces.

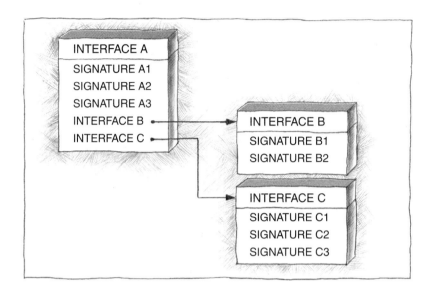

Here is a simple example of a message interface that deals with pricing. In this illustration, prices can be set and can be requested. Who sets a price and how it is determined doesn't matter to the interface; all that matters is how the price is communicated to an object and how the object reports that price back. An interface to support these minimal services would be the pair of message signatures shown in the accompanying figure.

Example: priced objects

A pricing interface

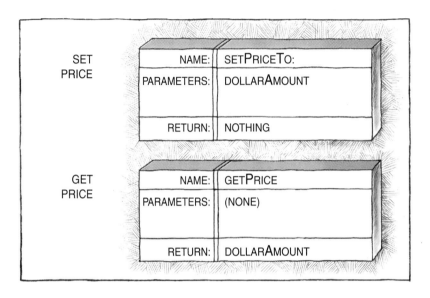

Most interfaces are much richer than this

Although some interfaces are as simple as this two-message, get-and-set interface, most interfaces contain a richer set of methods than this. Pricing offers a good opportunity to explore some of this richness because pricing is one of the most complex aspects of business. The *PricedObject* interface could readily be extended to include handling discount terms, discount schedules, special sales, and many other factors that influence price. Each of these factors would require supporting messages, so the *PricedObject* interface could easily contain a dozen or more message signatures.

Interfaces are independent of implementation

Once defined, this interface can be attached to any object that can be assigned a price. Using this standard interface automatically assures that all *PricedObjects* communicate properly with objects representing sales people, customers, contracts, sales orders, line items, accounts, and the myriad of other business entities that require or affect pricing information.

Defining Implementations

The first rule of implementation is that the service interface defined by a class must be fully satisfied. This means that every message signature contained in the interface must have a corresponding method that responds to this message. If the interface is composite, then the messages contained in its component interfaces must also be implemented. Methods are defined by writing procedures that make use of the parameters passed in as part of the message and return the appropriate kind of response.

Every message needs a method

As these methods are being developed, operations may be discovered that are generic in that they can be called into action by more than one method of the class. Such operations should be defined as separate methods in order to make them available to all other methods of the object. For example, the developer of a *Part* class may find that two or more messages may require ordering more of the part. In this case, the developer should define an internal *reorder* method that can be called by any method requiring this service.

Internal methods may also be defined

A common *reorder* method

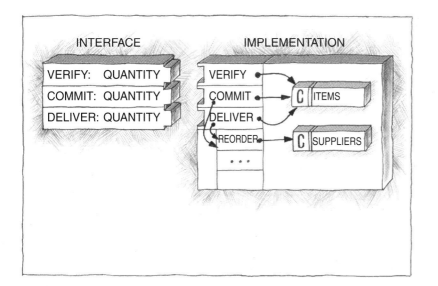

Variables are defined as needed	As the methods of a class are programmed, many of them will be found to require storage for intermediate results. If these results are required only during the time the method is executing, they can be placed in temporary variables that go away when the method completes its work. If the results need to be retained after the method has finished execution or if they need to be accessed by other methods in the class, then they are stored in named variables. The next section examines how these variables are defined and managed.

Defining Variables

Variables usually have declared types	As variables are identified and named, they are also assigned a type that describes the kind of information they will hold. When variables are intended to hold basic data types such as letters and numbers, there is no question about how the type should be defined. If a variable is going to hold a string of characters, you declare it to be of type *string* and be done with it.
Typing objects can be done in two ways	The process of typing becomes more interesting when variables hold references to other objects. If a *Call* object contains a *Rater* object as a component, that component must truly be able to perform the operations of rating a telephone call or the system will malfunction with the first call that is placed! As with parameters, there are two options for declaring the types of variables: classes and interfaces.
Classes can be used as constraints	The most common approach historically has been to constrain a variable by specifying a class as its type, allowing only instances of that class and its subclasses to occupy the variable at execution time. This approach has the same benefits and limitations discussed in the preceding chapter. It offers a certain level of generality, but it constrains objects to a single branch of the class hierarchy.

The second option is to use message interfaces to specify the types of objects that variables can reference. The advantages of this approach are the same as with parameters. That is, any object that satisfies the interface can occupy the variable, regardless of where it appears in the class hierarchy, and the communications with the object are constrained to the specified interface. Here again, the trend in object design is toward the use of interfaces instead of classes to specify the types of objects.

Interfaces offer more flexibility

For example, many different kinds of objects might be involved in selling products. If the variables in these objects are constrained to hold an instance of the *Product* class or one of its subclasses, then we can be assured that all the objects involved in selling will be talking to an object that knows how to tell us a price, transfer ownership, and perform other functions related to sales. But suppose you decide to sell off some used equipment or an unprofitable business unit. These are not products, so none of the objects involved in sales will be able to reference them as the object of a sale.

Example: selling products

The alternative is to declare an interface called something like *sellableObject* that contains the signatures for all the messages relating to the process of selling something. Naturally, the *Product* class will implement this interface from the outset. But the *Equipment* and *BusinessUnit* classes probably won't. That's no problem—just add the *sellableObject* interface to the class of any object you want to sell and define appropriate implementations for each of the methods. Having done that, all objects within your company that pertain to sales will accept equipment, business units, or anything else you want to sell.

A sellableObject interface solves the problem

Specialization Hierarchies

Arranging Classes in Hierarchies

Inheritance can span multiple levels

Inheritance is not limited to a single level but will cascade down any number of levels in a class hierarchy. This makes inheritance a very powerful mechanism because classes can be endowed with rich sets of capabilities simply by placing them in the correct branch of a class hierarchy. They automatically pull together all the interface and implementation definitions of the classes above them in the hierarchy, defining for themselves only the additional capabilities that make them unique.

This leads to efficient packaging of information

The class hierarchy is a very efficient mechanism because you can use method and variable definitions in more than one subclass without duplicating their definitions. For example, consider a system that represents various kinds of human-operated vehicles. This system would contain a generic class *Vehicle*, with subclasses for all the specialized types. The *Vehicle* class would contain the methods and variables that were pertinent to all vehicles, such as those for dealing with identification numbers, passenger loads, and fuel capacity. The subclasses, in turn, would contain any additional methods and variables that were specific to the more specialized cases.

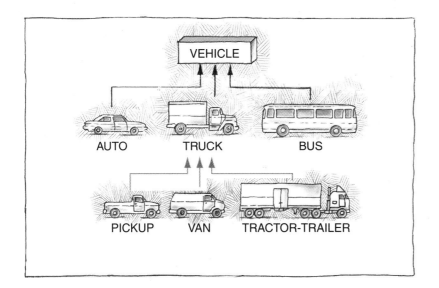

The ability to capture general cases in high-level classes is so useful that designers of object systems often define high-level classes purely for organizational purposes, even though no instances of those classes will ever exist. Such classes are known as **abstract classes**. For example, there are no instances of the *Vehicle* class just discussed—any object that would qualify as a vehicle is actually an *Automobile*, a *Truck*, an *Aircraft*, or some other particular kind of vehicle. But defining the general class *Vehicle* brings a higher level of organization to the class hierarchy, and it provides a convenient place to put all the methods and variables that apply to vehicles as a group.

Some classes are purely organizational

Method Mobility

Classes aren't affected by method origins

One consequence of how inheritance works is that classes are completely insensitive to where inherited definitions are actually defined. This allows object developers a great deal of freedom to move these definitions around within the hierarchy without affecting the operation of lower-level objects. To draw from two prior examples, suppose you had already developed two of the class hierarchies described earlier: one for automated vehicles and another for human-operated vehicles, as shown in the accompanying figure.

Two separate vehicle hierarchies

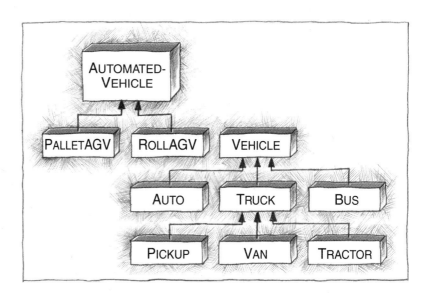

Example: combining two hierarchies

As these two hierarchies mature and gain increased abilities, you discover that you are duplicating a lot of code. You decide to combine the two hierarchies into a single hierarchy in order to eliminate the duplication and have a single point of change. Your new, combined hierarchy is to look like the one in the accompanying figure.

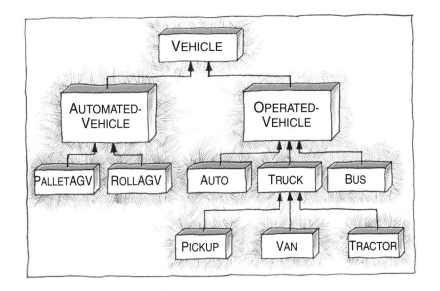

Notice that your *Vehicle* class is now the superclass for vehicles of all kinds and that there is a new *OperatedVehicle* class that brings together what used to be its immediate subclasses. Because *Vehicle* is now playing a more general role, you would need to take any definitions that pertain to a human operator (such as authorizing operation and identifying the current operator) out of *Vehicle* and move them down into the *OperatedVehicle* class. In addition, you would need to move definitions that characterize all vehicles (such as current location and destination) up into the *Vehicle* class.

Definitions would have to be moved around

How would these changes affect, say, the *RollAGV* and *Van* classes? The answer: Not at all. They still pull together the same sets of definitions. Since they have no information about where these definitions came from, they are completely unaffected by these movements. The fact that classes don't depend on the locations of their inherited definitions is yet another source of flexibility in object systems. As designers discover greater degrees of generalization and specialization among their classes, they are free to move definitions up and down the hierarchy at will.

These moves do not affect lower-level classes

Favoring Special Cases

Methods can be defined on multiple levels

Although methods are normally defined at only one level of a class hierarchy—the level at which they apply most generally—there is nothing to prevent a method from being defined at a general level and also at a more specific level. In this case, the inheritance mechanism always applies the more specific definition because that definition reflects the greater degree of specialization expressed by a subclass.

This technique helps define special cases

The ability to define methods on more than one level is typically used to create exceptions to general rules. Suppose you have a *Vehicle* class that includes a method *scheduleMaintenance* for setting up maintenance work based on time, mileage, and other factors. At a later date, your company acquires a private aircraft, so you create a new subclass of *Vehicle* called *Aircraft*. But now you have a problem: Scheduling maintenance for an aircraft is an entirely different process from the procedure you've been using for all your ground-based vehicles.

Adding an *Aircraft* subclass

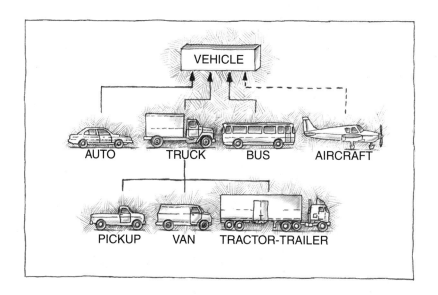

62

One way to fix your class hierarchy would be to move the *schedule-Maintenance* method down a level into the subclasses for the various types of vehicle. But this approach would require you to modify the *Vehicle* class and all of its subclasses. More importantly, all but one of the vehicle classes would wind up containing identical methods for scheduling maintenance, and that wouldn't be very efficient.

Changing existing classes isn't a good solution

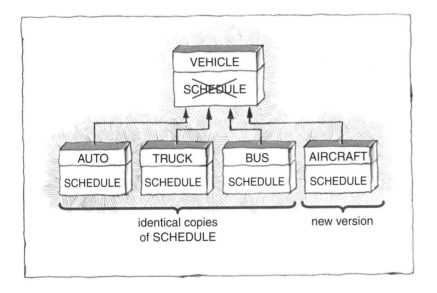

Moving scheduling down (inefficient solution)

The best way to fix the hierarchy is just to redefine *scheduleMaintenance* in the *Aircraft* class to handle its special maintenance needs. Then, you have only two versions of the method: one in the *Vehicle* class that handles the general case and the other down in the *Aircraft* class that handles the one exception. This solution is more efficient, and it doesn't require you to make any changes to your existing classes. Moreover, if you later change the way maintenance is scheduled for ground vehicles, you only have to modify the method in one location.

Redefining the method locally is more efficient

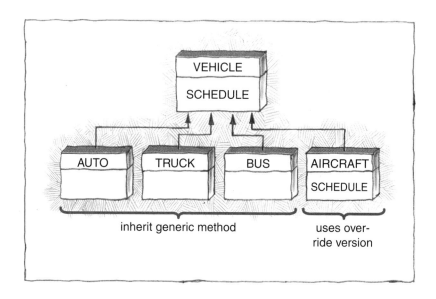

Redefining aircraft scheduling (efficient solution)

inherit generic method

uses override version

This technique is called overriding

This technique of redefining a method in a subclass is another example of polymorphism, where the same method name is used in two different classes. In this particular case, where one of the classes is a subclass of the other, the technique is called **overriding** because the method in the subclass overrides the more general version.

Overriding mirrors the way people learn

Overriding is an important technique because it allows special cases to be handled efficiently and easily, with minimal impact on other objects. This technique also happens to reflect the way people learn and retain information, building up general rules wherever possible and then overriding them with special cases as needed. This is yet another way in which the object approach conforms to our natural way of looking at the world. It also provides another example of the adaptability of object systems. If you need a singular exception to the general rule of a class, just override the required methods in a subclass.

5

Objects as Software Components

Object technology is not just another variety of programming language—it is a grand opportunity to redefine the entire process of software construction. The pioneers of commercial objects envisioned an industrial revolution for software that would bring an end to the handcrafting of monolithic applications and replace it with the assembly of software systems from pluggable components. This is a magnificent vision, but, of all the promises of object technology, it appears to be the furthest from being realized. This chapter takes a critical look at both the potential and the problems of objects as software components. The conclusions that result are a prescription both for corporate developers and the object industry as a whole.

A New Industrial Revolution

In Chapter 1, I argued that we need to set higher goals for objects rather than simply improving the construction of conventional applications. After 50 years of slow, incremental improvements in development tools and techniques, it's time to recognize that the accepted approach to software development is no longer adequate to provide timely business solutions. We need a revolutionary change.

We need a better way to build software

As it happens, we once faced a situation very much like this one in the construction of material goods. Like software construction, this problem also resisted incremental approaches to improvement. It required nothing less than a fundamental revolution in our thinking about how we create physical products. This revolution is now regarded as one of the great turning points in human history. It is known as the Industrial Revolution.

We need a new Industrial Revolution

Handcrafting Products

Material goods used to be entirely hand-crafted

Just 200 years ago, there was no manufacturing as we know it today. Products were created one at a time by highly trained crafts-men who learned their trade through long apprenticeship. Individual craftsmen were each responsible for creating complete products, and they enjoyed considerable latitude in the way they plied their trade. Each product bore the unique stamp of the person who made it, and each was, in a very real sense, a work of art.

Example: the fabrication of a rifle

A gunsmith, for example, created a rifle completely from scratch, starting with blocks of wood and pieces of iron. Each part was carefully fabricated to fit an individual weapon. Every screw was cut from rod stock, individually threaded, and hand fitted to the pieces it would fasten together. A finished rifle might have the same general design as other rifles in its class, but each one was unique in its details and performance.

Handcrafting a rifle

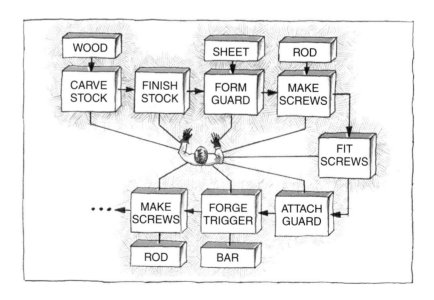

There is something aesthetically pleasing about this approach to the creation of material goods, and handcrafted products may be highly valued for their beauty and uniqueness. But the approach left much to be desired for an emerging industrial society. Individual crafting was painstakingly slow; the quality of output was inconsistent; the approach was very expensive; and it was nearly impossible to scale the process up to the level of mass production. Moreover, there was no way to standardize performance, and maintaining products in the field was often impossible because only the original craftsmen could repair their creations. If these symptoms sound familiar, read on!

This is not an efficient approach to production

The Industrial Revolution

In 1798, inventor Eli Whitney conceived a new way of building rifles that led to the modern form of manufacturing. The central concept behind Whitney's approach was to assemble rifles out of standard parts that could be interchanged freely among the individual weapons. Specialists made each type of part, and rigorously defined standards ensured that these parts were physically identical. Other specialists assembled the parts and tested the final product.

Eli Whitney developed a new approach

Mass-producing rifles

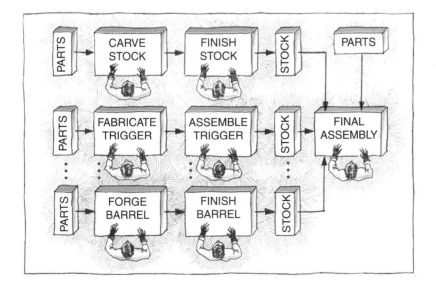

*This approach had
many advantages*

Whitney had to solve numerous technical and social problems be-fore he could put his idea into practice, but eventually his efforts were rewarded. Rifles could be produced much faster; overall quality was considerably improved; the cost of each weapon was greatly reduced; and the techniques scaled well to mass production levels. In addition, the weapons not only were more consistent in their performance but also were far easier to maintain because damaged rifles could be repaired using standard techniques and re-placement parts.

*Whitney caused a
paradigm shift*

Whitney's approach was not a refinement of existing methods but a radical departure from an accepted way of thinking—something historians call a **paradigm shift**. A **paradigm** is a view of the world that is based on assumptions so ingrained that they are rarely questioned, such as the assumption that individual gun-smiths build complete weapons. A paradigm shift requires raising those assumptions to consciousness, developing a new approach based on different assumptions, refining the approach until it works better than the old way, and making the social adjustments necessary to gain acceptance for the new approach. Paradigm shifts are rarely quick, easy, or pleasant.

Handcrafting Programs

*Software develop-
ment is still a craft*

Now, 200 years after the Industrial Revolution, the craft approach to producing material goods seems hopelessly antiquated. Yet this is precisely how we create software today. Each program is a unique creation, constructed piece by piece out of the raw materi-als of a programming language by skilled software craftspeople. Each component is fabricated specifically for the role it will play in its particular program and can rarely be used in the construction of other programs.

In short, conventional programming is roughly on par with manufacturing two centuries ago. Software development is painstakingly slow; the quality of software varies tremendously; the approach is very expensive; and the process does not scale well to large systems. Moreover, because each program is unique, standardization is impossible, and maintenance by anyone other than the original authors of a program is extremely difficult.

The results are typical of craft production

This comparison with the Industrial Revolution reveals the transition we must make in software development. Our goal should not be the evolutionary refinement of our existing process for software development, but a fundamental revolution in the way we build systems. Meeting this goal requires that we question all our implicit assumptions about how business systems are built, giving up our most ingrained ideas if necessary to transform the way we build these systems. We must have the courage and stamina to do what Whitney and his colleagues did—to undertake a true paradigm shift.

We need an industrial revolution for software

Making Software Components Work

Waiting for the Revolution

To date, object technology has not yet brought about the expected paradigm shift. It has provided substantial benefits to software developers, and those benefits have led to its widespread adoption. But it has not yet sparked a revolution. Twenty-five years after the invention of objects, programmers are still handcrafting new applications line by line. The only difference is that they are using objects instead of subroutines.

The revolution hasn't happened yet

To be fair to the effort, it *is* possible to buy reusable objects and plug them into new applications. But the objects available on the market today are mostly low-level utilities such as user interface components, database access tools, and communication interfaces. There is very little in the way of high-level business objects, and the cost of integrating these objects typically outweighs the benefits. The open, thriving market for pluggable business objects is still just a vision of the future.

*We should not be
surprised by this
delay*

Many people in the object industry are disappointed that the revolution has not yet occurred, but a further exploration of paradigm shifts suggests that we shouldn't be surprised. The term "paradigm shift" has become an industry buzzword that, like most buzzwords, has lost most of its original meaning. It is now most often used as a way of communicating just how great object technology is, which is rather like arguing that major surgery is much better than minor surgery. This loss of meaning is unfortunate because a real understanding of paradigm shifts is our best hope of surviving this one!

Paradigm shifts are always slow and painful. The one Eli Whitney precipitated took over 50 years to move through the full cycle of questioning, invention, refinement, and adoption. It is important to understand that each of these phases typically takes longer than the last. Once the right questions have been asked, the invention of a new approach may occur as a sudden insight. The subsequent refinement of that invention into a scalable, cost-effective business solution usually requires many years and much trial and error. The adoption process is typically slower still—it accounted for the great majority of the half century required by the Industrial Revolution.

As to the paradigm shift in software development, I believe that we are still in the refinement stage. Although much progress has been made in defining standards, it is still difficult to build business objects that are easily plugged together into working systems. Ironically, some of the characteristics that make objects powerful, such as inheritance, also make them difficult to use as pluggable components. Bear in mind that Whitney and his staff spent many years developing tools and techniques to produce interchangeable parts. Similarly, we need effective, standard techniques for producing and distributing business objects before the market for these objects can truly take off.

We are still in the refinement stage

Buying a Library for a Book

A look at the distribution system for objects reveals one of the fundamental obstacles to a software revolution. The way you buy objects today is by purchasing **class libraries**, which are groups of classes that perform related functions. This means that you can't buy just one class—even if you want only a single class from a library, you have to buy the entire library. Moreover, you can't use just the one class even after you own the library. The problem is that the class you want requires other classes in the library in order to function properly. Those classes, in turn, require still other classes, and so on.

We distribute classes in libraries

A web of class dependencies

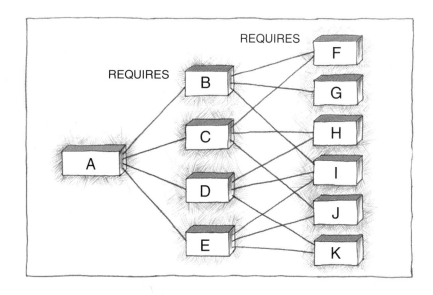

Libraries are hard to combine

The result of these dependencies is that using a single class from a library usually requires you to import the entire library of classes, few of which happen to match the requirements of your project. Worse yet, class libraries often provide overlapping but conflicting class definitions, making it nearly impossible to combine anything other than very low-level libraries.

This is not how real libraries work

The term "class library" is obviously an analogy with book libraries, but the analogy is a poor one. In a real library, you can check out a single book and read it in isolation. Any background knowledge required to understand this book can be drawn from whatever sources you choose: your existing knowledge, explanations from colleagues, other books and articles, or even a search of the Web. If real libraries worked like class libraries, you wouldn't have that flexibility. In order to read a single book, you would have to take home a dozen other books it depended on, each of which would require you to take another dozen books, until you wound up trucking the entire library home!

Fortunately, the increasing use of message interfaces to specify types offers a neat solution to this problem. If dependencies between objects are specified in terms of interfaces rather than classes, you are free to mix and match classes in any way you like so long as all their requirements are met. If you buy a *Product* class that requires that four different interfaces be satisfied, you can buy classes that satisfy those interfaces from four other vendors or build any number of them yourself. All your options are open.

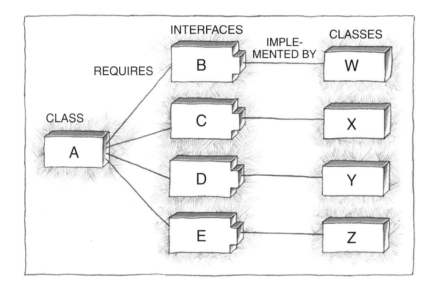

Ironically, there actually *is* a thriving market for software components, and it is thriving precisely because it relies on interfaces to connect components together. This is the approach taken by Microsoft with its VBX (Visual Basic) and ActiveX components. The fact that these components are not fully object-oriented does nothing to detract from their immense utility and commercial success.

The idea of connecting objects through interfaces has not been lost on the object community. In 1989, the **Object Management Group (OMG)**, the consortium charged with bringing order to the object industry, began its efforts by establishing a universal **Interface Definition Language (IDL)** for its **Common Object Request Broker Architecture (CORBA)**. The IDL specification allows objects from different vendors written in different languages to interact without any knowledge of one anothers' classes. Although a great step forward, this interface mechanism was designed primarily for remote communications and is generally not used among objects in the same execution space. The use of interfaces is only now being embraced for communications within object programs.

Dealing with Inheritance

The use of interfaces can eliminate most but not all class dependencies. Variables, parameters, and other object references can be typed by interface rather than class because no implementation information is required for these references. But this is not the case with subclassing, which is specifically designed to permit the inheritance of implementations as well as interfaces. In this case, there is no alternative but to specify a class. An interface just won't do the job.

One way of dealing with this exception is to simply get rid of inheritance. This is what Microsoft did with its **Component Object Model (COM)** technology, which underlies its VBX and ActiveX objects. This is also Microsoft's rationale for why it doesn't include inheritance in its view of object technology. Although this omission means that Microsoft's COM objects aren't truly object-oriented, it has also made it easier for the company to create a huge market for reusable software components.

Is Microsoft right? Should we sacrifice the power and elegance of class hierarchies to achieve truly pluggable components? My own view is that we would give up too much if we made that sacrifice. If other forms of class dependence are eliminated, inheritance has very little impact on the pluggability of object components. In fact, most ActiveX components are written in C++, and it is common practice to use inheritance internally to get code reuse across the various components in a package. This use of inheritance is simply hidden from view in the final product so that the components are able to function independently of one another.

There is a less dra-conian alternative

This same technique can easily be used in class libraries without hiding the use of inheritance. If we extract a single class from a library, it will automatically bring its superclasses with it in order to provide all the functionality it inherits. The visibility of the super-classes is merely a matter of packaging. The same set of method and variable definitions is extracted in any case. So, the COM approach appears to be a case of throwing the baby out with the bathwater. It is both technically and commercially feasible to build and market pluggable object components without sacrificing inheritance.

There is no need to hide inheritance

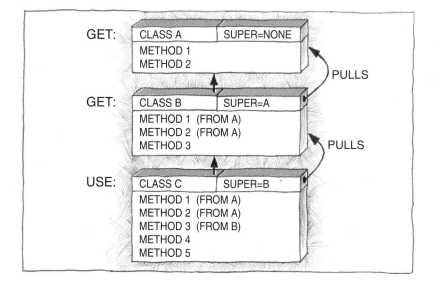

A class "summarizing" its inherited implementa-tions

The best approach to managing inheritance is to use it in moderation. The most important rule is to use inheritance only when one object is truly a special case of another. If you merely want an object to use the services of another object, then make the second object a component of the first, reference it through an interface, and delegate tasks to it. Only use inheritance where your business judgment tells you that one object really is a special kind of another.

Here is an example to clarify the distinction. If you have a class hierarchy for machines and another for capital assets, it might be tempting to make *Machine* a subclass of *CapitalAsset* so that it inherits the appropriate accounting behavior. However, that approach not only grafts two hierarchies together but also grafts two concepts together in a way that decreases flexibility. For example, there may be many kinds of machines, such as mixers or drills, that are not expensive enough to be treated as capital assets. The better approach is to attach an instance of *CapitalAsset* as a component of each *Machine* that qualifies for capital asset treatment. The *Machine* can then delegate to its *CapitalAsset* object all of the tasks related to depreciation, investment deductions, and other accounting behavior.

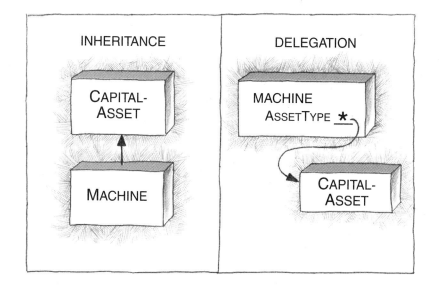

INHERITANCE

CAPITAL-
ASSET

MACHINE

DELEGATION

MACHINE
ASSETTYPE *

CAPITAL-
ASSET

Using delegation instead
of inheritance

Building the Right Components

Beyond the Manufacturing Analogy

In some respects, the problems we face in the software industry are much easier than those confronted by Eli Whitney. The ability to produce large volumes of identical software components, for example, is trivial. Once a class has been defined, all instances of that class are guaranteed to be identical in form and to function precisely as specified by the class. Objects can be produced in any quantity; they can be generated almost instantaneously; they consume no raw materials; and the manufacturing costs are negligible. This is a manufacturer's dream come true!

Reliable production is not a problem

A class manufacturing instances

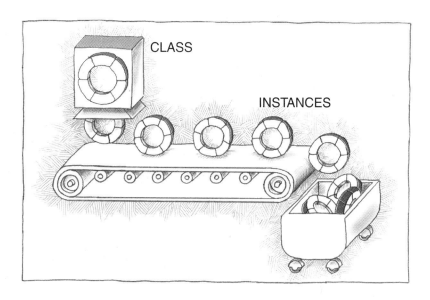

CLASS

INSTANCES

The challenge lies in engineering

The challenge of applying Whitney's method to software construction is not on the production side but on the engineering side. This distinction has important implications for how we view the problem. If we take the analogy too literally, it leads us back into conventional thinking.

Engineering goals are different

The goals for engineering and manufacturing are fundamentally different. The following argument for adopting object technology illustrates this point: We have to produce software faster; it's faster to assemble components than it is to create new software from scratch; therefore, we should build components that can be quickly configured to create new applications as needed. The reasoning is valid, but it is based on the implicit assumption that the goal is to produce software faster.

Paradigm shifts result from questioning such implicit assumptions. The result of my own questioning, as described in Chapter 1, is that adaptivity is far more important than productivity. If we can build business systems that are capable of continuous evolution over many years, there will be no need to keep writing new applications to solve each new business problem.

Adaptivity is better than productivity

Modeling the Elements of Business

If we are to build truly adaptive software systems to support our companies, we must design our components for longevity. This means modeling the fundamental elements of the business rather than creating objects that exist only to solve a current problem of the business. The examples in this book illustrate the kinds of components that are worthy of long-term investment—objects that represent products, customers, orders, shipments, payments, and other enduring elements of business. If well designed, such components can give many years of service, evolving gracefully as requirements change.

Components should model the business

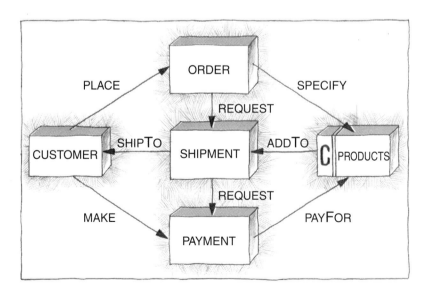

Components modeling a business

This is the strength
of object technology

Are objects well suited to modeling real-world business objects and their interactions? After all, the interactions among these objects can be extremely complex and difficult to represent accurately, much less execute faithfully. The answer to this question lies in the origins of objects. Object technology was originally conceived as a tool for simulating the behavior of complex, real-world systems. There is no better tool for the job.

6

Storing and Sharing Objects

The first five chapters of this book explain how to use objects to construct more adaptive programs. But as the software construction primer in the appendix points out, programming represents only half the problem—we must also address the issue of storing and sharing data across programs and their users. This is not an easy issue to resolve because object technology greatly expands the meaning of the term "data." In addition to the usual data types, objects can contain methods, complex data structures, multimedia information, references to other objects, and other kinds of data that are not easily stored in conventional databases. This chapter examines two options for dealing with these new requirements: extending the capabilities of existing database technologies and developing new database technologies specifically to meet the needs of objects.

The Problem of Persistence

Object programs rarely throw their objects away when the program stops running. Much more commonly, a program builds and maintains objects over time, reusing them whenever the program runs. Such objects are known as **persistent objects**. But where are these persistent objects kept when they are not in use? Where do objects go when their programs aren't running?

Most programs need to store objects

One way to store objects is to keep them in data files. A program transfers the contents of its objects out to a file as part of its shutdown procedure and then loads them back in again the next time it is run. In effect, the program disassembles the objects to pack them into the data file and then reassembles them when the program resumes.

Persistent objects can be stored in files

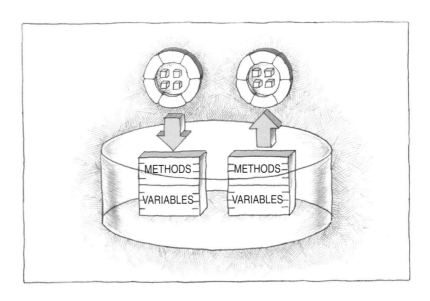

Storing Objects in Databases

*Sharing objects re-
quires a database
manager*

Storing objects in files works fine so long as no two people need to access the same objects at the same time. Otherwise, conflicts can arise because there is no "traffic cop" to check on who is working with which objects at any given moment. In addition, data files have no security mechanisms to control access to individual objects and no procedures for protecting the objects against loss. These are the same concerns that led to the development of database managers for storing persistent data, and the conclusion is the same in the case of objects: Shared persistent objects must be maintained by a **database management system (DBMS)**.

*Objects call for spe-
cial capabilities*

The next logical question is what *kind* of DBMS should be used? This question is the source of much confusion and controversy. Objects place special demands on DBMSs, and not all systems are suited to managing objects. Here are just a few of the ways that storing objects stretches the capabilities of data management systems:

1. Most object-oriented business designs make extensive use of composite objects and complex patterns of interactions among objects. This practice requires that DBMSs be able to store rich webs of object references and trace those references quickly and easily.

   Complex structures

2. The ability to define objects in terms of classes in inheritance hierarchies also creates new requirements for storage management. DBMSs must be able to store an inheritance hierarchy, reconstruct instances of classes using the information contained in the hierarchy, and handle changes to that hierarchy.

   Inheritance

3. Object technology encourages the definition of new kinds of objects, including such diverse forms as diagrams, pictures, X rays, video sequences, and sound recordings. This requires a DBMS that can store an infinitely expandable range of digital information.

   Multimedia information

4. Objects contain methods as well as data. This requires that a database be capable of storing programming code along with data and maintaining the cohesion between the two.

   Methods

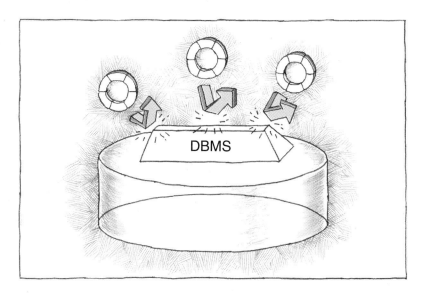

Trying to store objects in a standard database

There are many other requirements

This brief list barely scratches the surface of a very deep subject. On a more technical level, the efficient storage and retrieval of objects requires new kinds of concurrency controls (such as object-level locking rather than record-level locking), new kinds of access controls (based on the abilities of objects rather than the contents of tables), new optimization techniques (such as placing nested objects in the same storage unit on a disk drive), and dozens of other specializations. However, the four requirements just listed are the ones with the most direct business implications, so they are the focus of this chapter.

Using Conventional DBMSs

Simple objects are easily stored

Storing objects that are composed only of basic data types such as numbers, dates, and strings is relatively easy with conventional databases. The common practice of using object languages with relational databases works quite well with this kind of object. Each class defines a table, and each instance is represented as a row in that table. Storing and retrieving objects under these conditions is fast and efficient because it requires nothing more than storing and retrieving rows in tables, which is what relational databases were designed to do.

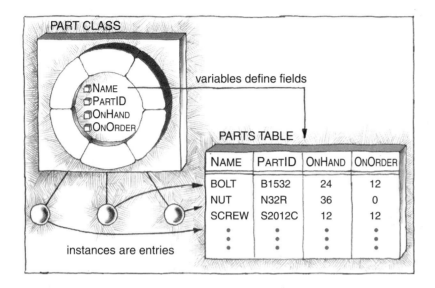

When objects are composed of other objects, difficulties begin to arise. Hierarchic and network databases, with their rich data structures and navigational access mechanisms, are very well suited to storing complex structures among objects. However, their inherent rigidity poses a serious problem—shutting down the database every time you modified a class could quickly bring your company to a standstill. Relational systems can handle these nested structures, but their use of associative access makes the process of storing composite objects painfully slow—often 100 to 1,000 times slower than databases that provide navigational access.

Composite objects are harder to store

Conventional databases were deployed before the mechanism of inheritance was widely used, and it is difficult to represent the relationships among objects defined in class hierarchies. Consider a class *RollAGV* that inherits variable definitions from its superclass *AutomatedVehicle* that, in turn, inherits variables from its superclass *Vehicle*. The table holding instances of *RollAGV* must either contain replicated definitions for the inherited variables or hold links to entries in the tables holding variables for the two superclasses. The first option is inflexible because any change in the variables of *Vehicle* would have to be replicated in the table for every subclass. The second option is more flexible but requires a time-consuming reconstruction of the object from multiple tables whenever it is retrieved from the database.

Storing an instance of
RollAGV

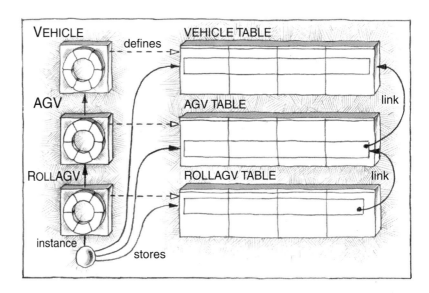

Multimedia data is rarely an option

Previous generations of database technology were designed for handling small sets of predefined data types such as numbers, dates, and strings. The kind of multimedia information used by objects is simply beyond them.

The need to store object methods rules out hierarchic and network models altogether as these make no provision for storing procedures. Relational systems do support stored procedures, so they are not at a complete loss in this regard. However, these procedures must usually be programmed in special data management languages such as SQL, which means that the methods normally used in object-oriented programs cannot be stored in relational DBMSs.

Method storage is extremely limited

In sum, it is possible to store objects in conventional databases, particularly relational systems, if the objects contain no multimedia information and methods can be saved using other mechanisms. However, network and hierarchic DBMSs are too rigid to provide a useful solution. Relational DBMSs offer more flexibility, but they become quite slow and cumbersome with objects that contain or inherit from other objects—conditions that are the rule rather than the exception with business objects. Object folklore has it that storing a complex object in a relational database is like disassembling your car into its component parts in order to put it in your garage. It's possible, but it's not a very efficient use of your time!

Conventional RDBMSs are not a good fit

A New Generation of Databases

A much simpler solution to the problem of storing objects is to use a new kind of database that is specifically designed to meet the requirements of object technology. Databases of this type are known as **object database management systems** (**ODBMSs**). Object databases offer a better way to store objects because they provide all the traditional database services while also meeting the special needs of object technology.

Object databases are built to hold objects

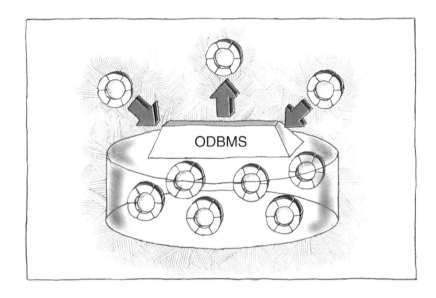

Managing Complex Structures

*Composite objects
support complex
structures*

In an object database, complex structures are represented by composite objects—that is, objects that contain other objects. These
component objects can contain other objects in turn, and so on, allowing structures to be nested to any degree.

*Composite objects
contain object refer-
ences*

Composite objects do not literally contain other objects, in the
sense that one object is physically stored inside the other. Rather,
composite objects contain the effective addresses of their component objects, allowing them to be accessed quickly when needed.
This same system of object references is also used for relationships
other than composition. As a result, the nested data structures of
an object database can imitate the more general form of the network database model rather than being restricted to the hierarchic
model.

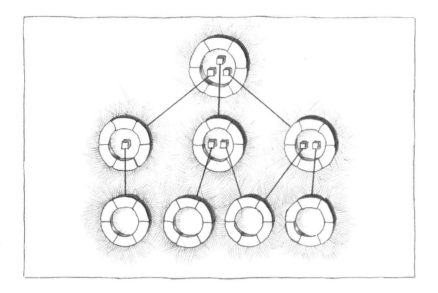

Object databases offer the fast navigational access of network and hierarchic databases that many companies gave up when they adopted relational databases. Object databases can restore navigational access without sacrificing flexibility because the navigational information isn't stored as a master pattern separate from the operational data, as it was in earlier generations of DBMS technology. Instead, it is recorded directly within each instance stored in the database. This means that changes can be made quickly and specialized patterns added on the fly without disturbing the operation of the database.

Object databases restore navigational access

The fact that object databases store navigational references as part of their data offers another advantage—it means that they can support any number of alternative structures for the same set of data. These alternative structures are not simply "views" of the data superimposed on a single underlying model, as in relational databases. All the structures are equally valid, and each one exists independently of the others. You can create new structures and modify old ones without affecting other structures in any way. In

Multiple structures can coexist

this regard, object databases go well beyond the structures of network databases, still without incurring any of the rigidity that characterizes these earlier systems.

Multiple structures in an object database

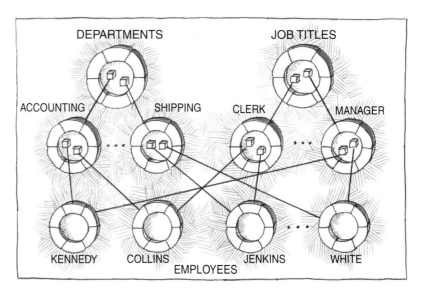

DEPARTMENTS   JOB TITLES

ACCOUNTING   SHIPPING   CLERK   MANAGER

KENNEDY   COLLINS   JENKINS   WHITE

EMPLOYEES

Object databases provide fast access

Object databases not only store complex structures with ease and flexibility, they also can retrieve those structures much more quickly because they are stored as direct references between objects rather than lookups based on content. To see how this works, consider the breakdown of a product into its component parts—what manufacturers call a bill of materials (BOM). A relational database would represent each product by a series of entries in a table that lists its components. Each of these components, in turn, would be defined by another series of entries, possibly in some other table. These subcomponents would be linked to still lower-level components, and so on, until the most elementary parts in the product were reached. A moderately complex product might require half a dozen levels of components with an average of, say, five components each, for a total of over 3,000 links. Each of these links would be formed by having a particular value—the part number in this case—appear in both entries.

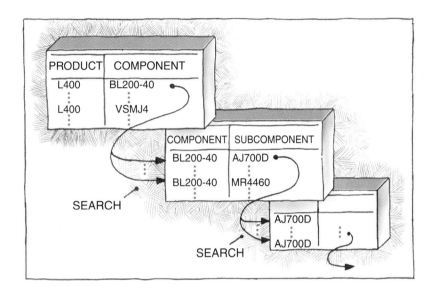

Retrieving this bill of materials from a relational database is a time-consuming process because the system must search the database each time it traces a link from one component to the next. If a component consists of parts BL200-40, VSMJ4, KS9000B, and MRG4400-D, then the database manager has to scan each of the appropriate tables to locate these part numbers. Relational databases are optimized to perform this kind of search quickly, but there is still a significant time penalty when thousands of searches are required to retrieve a single structure.

Retrieval based on content is slow

An object database stores a product as a composite object, with the links to its components represented as direct references. This representation allows the DBMS to navigate directly to the components on every level, quickly extracting the entire structure. To give you an idea of just how significant the performance improvements can be, an experiment conducted by the U.S. Navy showed an object database outperforming a relational system by three orders of magnitude (1,000 times faster!) on both storage and retrieval.

References make retrieval fast and efficient

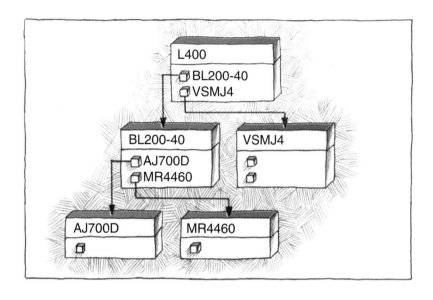

Support for Inheritance

Support for inheritance is built in

Built-in support for inheritance not only meets the needs of storing objects, it also brings an unprecedented level of flexibility to information storage. A common restriction imposed by conventional databases is that all entries of a given type must conform to the same structure. If new entries require a different structure, there are only two choices: force the new entries into the existing structure or define a new structure that includes the new requirements and convert all existing entries to fit it. Object databases offer a third choice: create a subclass to accommodate the exceptions, providing for the additional information without disturbing the existing entries.

Example: storing foreign addresses

Here is an illustration that demonstrates the advantages of subclassing. Many non-U.S. addresses require special designators to record townships, parishes, cantons, or other regional groupings. A company just beginning an overseas sales effort might find itself in the awkward situation of not being able to represent these addresses in its customer database. The company can't very well throw away the additional information. On the other hand, restructuring the database to accommodate the new entries is not a cost-effective solution. In addition to the time and cost of the programming effort required to change both the database and the programs that access it, restructuring wastes valuable storage space for all the domestic customers who don't use the added designator.

An object database solves the problem by subclassing the customer address class. The new subclass simply defines an extra variable to hold the additional information, inheriting all its other characteristics from the regular address class. No changes are required to existing customers, and nothing is wasted because entries for domestic customers don't set aside space for information they don't use.

Creating a subclass solves the problem

Special case of the address class

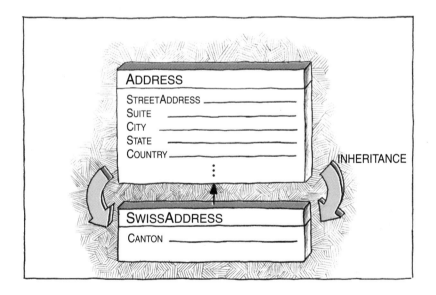

Multimedia and Method Storage

Object databases support multimedia

Conventional databases were conceived and designed when computers dealt almost exclusively with text and numbers, so it is not surprising that they have trouble with multimedia information. Today, computers operate directly on a wide range of media, including drawings, blueprints, photographs, video sequences, human speech, sound patterns, and many other forms. Object databases were conceived and constructed with the express goal of accommodating any kind of information that could be rendered in digital form. This provides the unbounded extensibility of data types required by object technology.

Storing multimedia information

Object databases can also store methods

Finally, most object databases have some facility for storing the methods of the objects they manage. However, this is one of the least developed areas of object databases, and it is not as widely used as the support for multimedia, inheritance, and complex structures. In some cases, the support for methods is nothing more than the ability to include the stored procedures of relational databases. Although useful, this capability is not nearly as powerful as the ability to store full class information, including the methods of objects in their original language.

Even for those object databases that permit true method storage, this feature is not often used by developers. In most cases, programmers continue to store their methods in code management systems such as **source code control systems** and **runtime libraries**. The most likely explanation for the failure to develop and use this feature of object databases is the continuing perception that object-oriented databases are just that—databases. Developers are simply not accustomed to storing programming code in databases, and ODBMS vendors have been slow to provide the full suite of functionality that would entice them into changing their ways.

Method storage is not often used

A Simpler Way to Work

There is a further advantage to object databases that can have a major impact on the success of development projects. On the programming side, objects allow you to think in terms of real-world business objects such as customers, products, sales, and shipments. When such objects are stored in RDBMSs, however, they must be disassembled into separate, independent tables. The result is a set of low-level data structures that bear little resemblance to the original objects, just as a garage full of parts would be hard to recognize as a car. This radical transformation introduces what is sometimes called a "semantic gap" between software developers and data managers. Developers think in terms of real-world business objects, whereas data managers think in terms of entries in data tables. The value of objects as tools for thinking about the business gets lost in the translation.

RDBMSs introduce barriers to thinking

**Transforming objects
into relational tables**

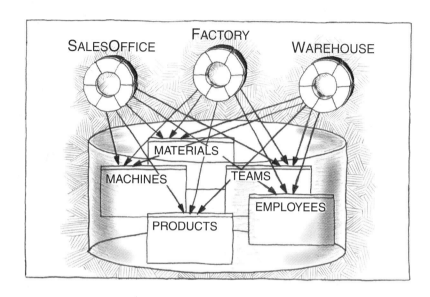

*ODBMSs eliminate
these barriers*

By eliminating this translation process, object databases allow developers and data managers to think in the same terms. Objects are stored intact in the database, and they retain their integrity as direct representations of the business. Programmers and data managers can think in the same terms, without losing shared meaning in a translation process. This direct mapping of objects between programs and databases greatly facilitates communication across two groups of people. It also allows objects to be changed much more easily because it eliminates the need to go through the object-to-relational mapping process with each change. And anything that eases change brings us closer to the goal of adaptive business systems.

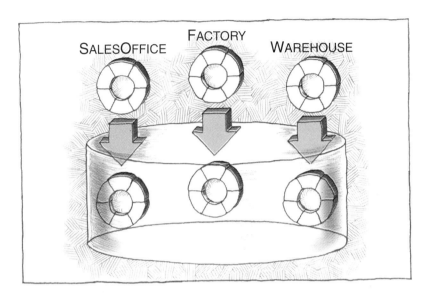

The Battle of the Generations

The use of object databases is now widespread, and the battle of the generations has been joined. The market is insisting on support for objects, and nearly all the major RDBMS vendors have proclaimed that their products will soon provide full support for objects. The question now is not whether to buy a DBMS that supports objects but when to buy it and from whom.

The future belongs to objects

As the vendors of ODBMSs are quick to point out, each new database technology has produced a new generation of vendors that rose to dominance, pushing aside the vendors of the older technology. In each case, existing vendors promised to extend their product with new features to fit the emerging model. In each case, products specifically designed to meet the new requirements have won out over the retrofitted models. The question at hand is whether history will repeat itself.

Next-generation vendors usually prevail

The Extended Relational Model

RDBMS vendors want to break the pattern

Naturally, the RDBMS vendors argue that this time around is different and that they can easily migrate their products to meet the needs of object technology. The solution they offer is formally known as the **extended relational DBMS**, although the term "object relational" is often used for marketing purposes. These vendors have made some progress in extending the relational model, but a full realization of this model has yet to appear on the market.

BLOBs hold multimedia information

The first extension to relational databases has been the incorporation of multimedia information. This is done through the addition of **binary large objects**, or **BLOBs**, as a new data type. Although BLOBs get the job done, the solution is about as elegant as the acronym suggests. Instead of having rich, extensible types based on subclasses, everything that isn't a basic data type is lumped into a single category, stored in an external file, and simply referenced in the database.

Navigation is being added for structure

A harder problem for RDBMSs is providing high-speed, navigational access. The first hurdle to overcome is the fact that direct links among data elements violate the fundamental principles underlying relational database theory. Fortunately for the RDBMS vendors, it has recently been "discovered" that such links don't violate the relational model after all and were actually an integral part of the model from its inception. So, the vendors are now free to provide navigational access. It remains to be seen how well they do that and how the performance of their systems compares with that of true object databases.

Inheritance and methods remain problems

Although RDBMS vendors are working on the problem of supporting inheritance in the relational model, the jury is still out on how well they can do this. As to methods, the relational vendors appear to be moving toward **OSQL**, an object-oriented version of SQL that provides better support for objects, but there is little indication that they plan to manage the actual methods of the objects that are stored.

It remains to be seen how well the extended relational model will handle the primary problems of storing objects. It is important to remember, however, that these are just four of the most visible problems that relational vendors must solve. There is also the myriad of lesser but critical technical features mentioned earlier, and these may ultimately make the difference between the success or failure of extended relational databases. The vendors of object databases have built their products from the ground up to handle the specialized needs of objects, and most of them now have a decade of refinement in commercial settings to tune their database engines. Given the difficulty of modifying large software systems such as DBMSs, it's hard to imagine achieving the same quality outcome by retrofitting existing systems.

The infrastructure may make the difference

Peaceful Coexistence

Although relational databases are not particularly good at storing objects, there are situations where they are the best choice. If your design consists primarily of shallow objects that contain more basic data types than references to other objects, an RDBMS can perform quite nicely. In this case, the mapping is carried out as described earlier, with each class defining a table and each instance being stored as a row in that table. Under these conditions, there is no significant performance penalty, and the well-known benefits of relational databases become more influential factors in your selection process.

Use RDBMSs for shallow objects

By contrast, if your design makes significant use of object nesting, cross-referencing, and inheritance, you should opt for an ODBMS. The usual reasons for choosing a relational system are simply overwhelmed by the awful performance you will get from the RDBMS, not to mention the time and cost required to write the conversion

Use ODBMSs for deep objects

software for mapping objects to relations. ODBMSs are now mature, robust, stable, scalable, and thoroughly proven in commercial applications. The net risk of *not* using an object database when your situation requires it usually outweighs any risks associated with adopting a newer-generation technology.

Plan on mixing database types

It should be clear from the preceding examples that you are unlikely to find a single DBMS that will be well suited for every situation in your company. While the desire to standardize on a single product is understandable, the costs of such a decision can easily outweigh the benefits. A particularly powerful combination is to use an object DBMS as a front-end to one or more relational systems. Most commercial ODBMSs offer transparent access to relational databases, allowing large volumes of shallow objects to be stored in relational databases while providing excellent support for complex objects that require navigational access. From the view of an object application, everything—including existing data in relational systems—automatically appears as objects.

Combining database types

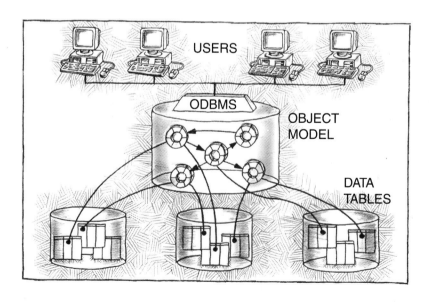

7

Beyond Programs and Databases

Up to this point, I have presented object technology within the framework of the conventional distinction between programs and databases described in the software construction primer in the appendix. It is now time, not just in this book but in the software industry itself, to look beyond that classic division of labor and explore the full impact of object technology on business systems. The most fundamental principle of object technology is the encapsulation of related procedures and data. The biggest obstacle to fully realizing that principle is the distinction between programs and databases. This chapter explores the tools and techniques necessary to tear down that barrier and enjoy the benefits of fully integrated business systems.

Integrating Procedures and Data

One of the most enduring assumptions underlying software development is the idea that procedures and data should be managed separately. Procedures are embedded in programs, and data is maintained in databases. This assumption is so ingrained in our collective thinking that it continues to dictate the architecture of business systems after 50 years of advances in hardware and software technology. The assumption is also arbitrary, antiquated, and antithetical to our emerging understanding of complex systems.

Procedures and data need not be separated

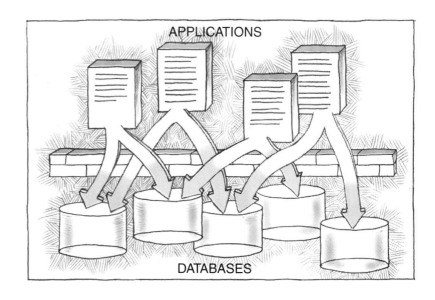

APPLICATIONS

DATABASES

Equal Treatment for Procedures

They are just two different kinds of information

Ultimately, procedures and data are just two different forms of information about a business. Procedures represent information about how the operations of the company are to be performed, and data represent information about the status of the company, including its recent and planned actions. We are accustomed to representing procedures as program code and data as values stored in data management systems, but this distinction is not carved in stone. Data can be expressed as formulas, which are really implicit procedures for calculating a value. And procedures can be expressed as data, as they are in table-driven 4GLs and script-driven workflow systems. Given the underlying commonality of intent between procedures and data, it is important to ensure that both kinds of information are managed appropriately in business systems.

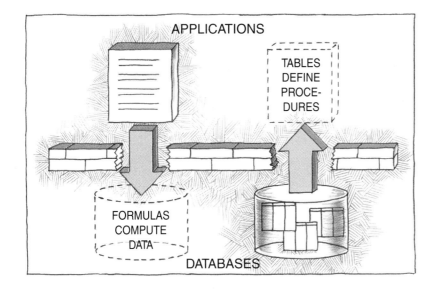

APPLICATIONS

TABLES
DEFINE
PROCE-
DURES

FORMULAS
COMPUTE
DATA

DATABASES

Crossing the barrier be-
tween data and proce-
dures

In the early decades of business computing, procedures were relatively stable, whereas data tended to change quite frequently.
Moreover, the kinds of procedures delegated to a computer, such
as billing and accounting calculations, tended to be pretty generic
across companies, whereas the data of each company was distinct
and proprietary. Given these differences, it is understandable that
the industry developed sophisticated, secure, enterprise-level systems for managing data, while developing relatively rudimentary,
nonsecure, localized technologies for managing code. To appreciate
the extent of the difference in the way we treat data and procedures, compare your corporate budget for database management
with the corresponding budget for "procedurebase" management.

*Data used to require
special management*

Procedures now require equal treatment

Over the years, the roles of procedures and data have changed dramatically. Procedures are no longer stable. In fact, the ability to change procedures quickly in response to changing business conditions is now a critical success factor. Moreover, the procedures entrusted to computers are no longer the simple, generic routines they once were. Superior business processes now represent the essence of competitive advantage, and these competitive practices are increasingly codified and executed in computer systems. Yet we still manage these systems as though data were the corporate jewels, to be protected behind the walls of high-powered DBMSs, while leaving the definitions of procedures lying around in relatively unprotected code files. I submit that it's time the treatment of procedures caught up with the new business realities.

Respecting Encapsulation

Object technology calls for equal treatment

One of the key characteristics of object technology is the equal treatment of data and procedures. Taken together, the principles of encapsulation and information hiding require not only that data and procedures be packaged together but also that the very distinction between the two be hidden within each object. If we are to fully leverage these principles, the two should never be separated from each other, much less treated differently.

Programs and databases violate encapsulation

Yet this is precisely what the separation between programs and databases does. Although programs may temporarily hold variables, their primary function is to execute procedures. Similarly, although databases may execute stored procedures, their primary function is to contain data. This separation of procedures and data represents a violation of encapsulation at the most fundamental level.

Encapsulation is not an idealistic principle that can readily be compromised in real-world situations. It is a pragmatic principle that has a profound impact on the effectiveness of business systems. Separating the management of procedures and data greatly limits the adaptivity of a system. The negative effects of this practice are felt every time a change is made to the structure of a database. When hundreds or even thousands of programs use a shared corporate database, the consequences of even a minor change in data structures can range from a major inconvenience to a full-scale disaster.

This violation has practical consequences

This problem isn't solved by the adoption of object databases. Mapping an object onto a database—be it relational or object-oriented—necessarily exposes the internal variables of the object. If you change the structure of the data defined in a class, you have to modify the structure of the database to reflect the change in the class. Then, you have to modify and redeploy every application that deals with instances of that class. All these changes must take effect at the same time, or serious errors will occur in the execution of the business. It doesn't matter what kind of database you choose. As long as you continue to treat procedures and data in different ways, the synchronization problem will always be with you, acting as a major impediment to organizational change.

Object databases perpetuate the problem

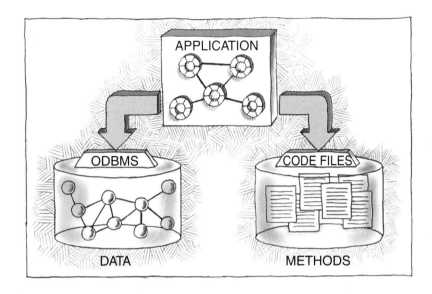

Separating data and methods for storage

For objects, the two must be merged

A full realization of object principles requires us to eliminate the distinction between programs and databases. This can only be done with a technology that seamlessly integrates the capabilities of the two. The next section introduces this technology.

The Evolution of Object Engines

We can combine programs and databases

The solution to the problem of merging programs and databases is a technology I call the **object engine**. Unlike object databases, which may record methods but do not execute them, object engines support fully active objects. They include all the functionality required to both store and execute objects within a concurrent, multiuser environment.

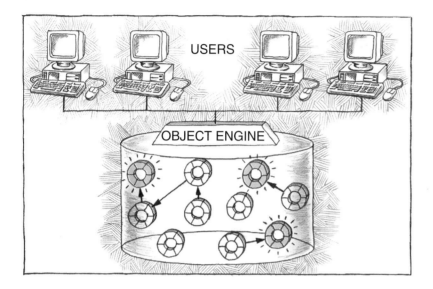

The object engine may sound like a radically new technology, but it has actually been on the market for more than a decade and is now being used in large-scale, production business systems. The reason you haven't heard about object engines before is that they have been masquerading as object databases. This is a story worth telling because it illustrates the depth of our resistance to managing procedures and data in a uniform, integrated environment.

Object engines are a proven technology

The first object databases delivered for commercial use were designed to provide full support systems for objects, including concurrent, multiuser execution as well as object storage. They were purchased primarily by research groups within large corporations, who spent most of their time trying to figure out what to do with

These engines started out as object databases

them. In the meantime, a second wave of object databases dropped the execution aspect and offered data storage only. Given the strong tradition of separating procedures and data, this second generation of products fit the expectations of the market better and were adopted more readily. Vendors of the first-generation products, which offered considerably more functionality, were hard-pressed to differentiate themselves.

Repositioning is generating new demand

Recently, vendors of these products have begun to reposition their offerings as multiuser "application servers" rather than mere databases. This is a much more apt description, although I prefer the more generic term "object engine" because it echoes the existing term "database engine" while avoiding any implication of conventional applications or client-server architectures. Whatever they are called, the distinguishing characteristic of these products is that they offer an environment that maintains the encapsulation of objects at all times, eliminating the classic problem of synchronizing data definitions between programs and databases. Vendors of these products are now enjoying rapid growth as the value of integrating storage and execution becomes more apparent.

GemStone and IBEX sell object engines

Because object engines have been disguised as databases for so long, you may have trouble distinguishing them from the pack. Two current products in this category are GemStone from GemStone Systems and ITASCA from IBEX. GemStone offers versions of its product for Smalltalk and Java. Objects managed by ITASCA are programmed in LISP, a language developed specifically for rule-based systems.

Buying one of these products is not your only option. If you prefer, you can buy a standard object DBMS and build a shared execution environment in front of it. However, this is a major undertaking. Unless you have a strong need for features that aren't available in a commercial product, you are probably better off buying this technology rather than building it.

You can also build your own engine

The End of Applications

Executable Business Models

Object engines are sometimes portrayed as a better medium for executing conventional business applications, as defined in the software construction primer. Although this view is reasonable as far as it goes, it doesn't go very far. If we simply combine all the programs and databases that make up our applications and dump them into an object engine, all we'll get is a denser packing of the software silos we have already been living with. Applications that weren't designed to work together won't start communicating any better just because they are sharing the same execution environment.

Engines invite application integration

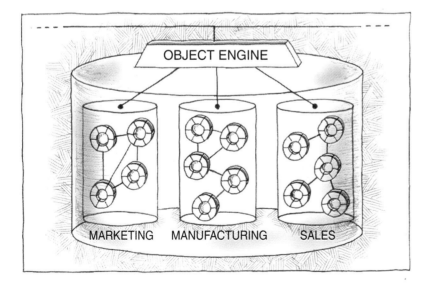

Software silos in an object engine

Object engines support executable business models

The key to getting the maximum leverage out of object engines is to use them to integrate the functions previously managed by distinct applications. Fortunately, there is a proven technique for achieving this goal. The surest way to build enduring systems that are capable of sustained evolution is to replace monolithic applications with dynamic, executable business models. Although simple in theory, this approach can be difficult in practice because it requires a scalable execution environment that can hold all the elements of a business model. Object engines offer an excellent platform for deploying these models.

Core processes can be executed in object engines

Because object engines provide a complete, multiuser execution environment, there's no limit to the scope and complexity of the operations an object engine can carry out. These operations enjoy special advantages over those that are isolated within conventional applications. For starters, functions executed in an object engine are available to all the users of a business system at all times, not just when a particular user is running a particular program. In fact, object engines can run 24 hours a day, carrying out routine tasks during the night even when no one is present.

Object models integrate disparate applications

Another advantage of object models is that they can integrate the information and behavior now managed by a multitude of incompatible applications. The key is to discover objects that cut across application boundaries and use them to integrate the functionality in these applications. Two good examples of this approach are *Product* and *Customer* objects. A brief look at each will illustrate the advantages of object models for integrating information and behavior, respectively.

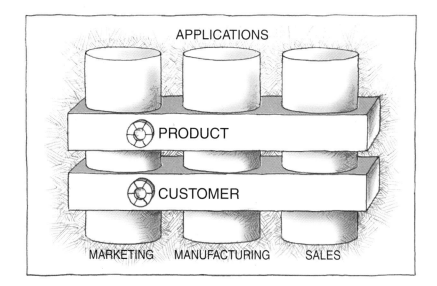

Integrating Information

Maintaining and using information about products offers a good opportunity to exploit this new approach. Today, companies maintain many different applications that deal with products. Each application addresses a different business problem; the applications tend to deal with different aspects of the product; and the set of applications communicate with one another either very badly or not at all. Sample applications include the following: product definition tools used in marketing; engineering applications that help design and specify products; manufacturing applications that plan and control production; pricing systems that establish base prices and apply discounts; sales applications that assist and track sales of products; and distribution applications that manage the physical distribution of products.

Product management is very complex

The problem of maintaining an integrated view of a product is so severe that yet another kind of application, the product information manager (PIM), has been developed just to collate key engineering and manufacturing information about a product. This kind of application layering is like using duct tape to hold baling wire in place—at some point, we have to stop patching "solutions" that don't work and remedy the underlying problem.

In this case, the problem is a fundamental lack of integration of the information pertaining to products. The cause of the problem is application thinking—the mindset that says that each business need should be addressed by a separate, stand-alone application. A deeper, more lasting solution is to design a single *Product* object that integrates all aspects of a product. This will undoubtedly be a complex object, with component objects for managing its complexity and multiple interfaces for presenting simplified sets of messages to marketing, sales, engineering, manufacturing, and distribution. But the *Product* object will ultimately act as a single point of reference for a particular product and also as a single point of change for that product.

A *Product* object integrating data

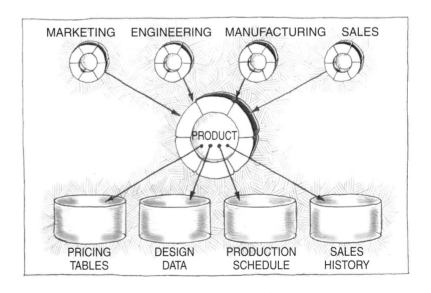

112

Integrating Behavior

For an example of how objects can integrate behavior, consider all
the various ways in which you interact with customers. Depending
on your business, you may profile customers demographically, sell
standard products to them, design custom products for them, ship
those products to specified locations, invoice them for their pur-
chases, collect payments, provide services, and project future sales
to them. In well designed conventional systems, these tasks are
each performed by a single application. More commonly, each task
is carried out by a variety of incompatible applications distributed
across the various regions in which you design, manufacture, sell,
and distribute products.

*Behavior should also
be integrated*

It is very difficult to get any kind of overview of your relationship
with your customers under these circumstances because each application maintains its own customer database. It is also very
difficult to coordinate your customer interactions because the
applications don't talk to one another. This lack of coordination
can lead to expensive business consequences. For example, it is not
uncommon for companies to sell incompatible products to their
customers through different distribution channels or to continue
selling products on credit to customers who are failing to pay for
what they have already purchased.

*Lack of integration
can be expensive*

Here again, the solution is to create a single *Customer* object that
pulls together all these related functions. As with the *Product* object, *Customer* will not be a simple object. It will have component
objects to help manage its complexity, and it will present different
interfaces to different parts of the organization. But all interactions
with a given customer flow through its corresponding *Customer* object, providing a single point of contact with the customer inside
the company. This object tracks all sales, collaborates with engineering and manufacturing regarding custom products, projects fu-

*A Customer object
coordinates interac-
tions*

ture sales based on previous sales and other information, dispatches services and records these, invoices the customer for all sales and services, and takes appropriate action when a customer fails to pay on time.

A *Customer* object integrating behavior

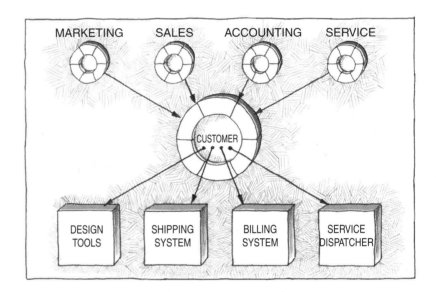

Leveraging Legacy Systems

Object integration is feasible

At this point, you may be thinking something along the lines of "Sounds great, but it's not going to happen in my lifetime." Here are a couple of observations to suggest that this kind of integration is more feasible than it might first appear.

You are already doing all the work

First, your company is already performing all the individual tasks—you just don't have any way to integrate them because they are taking place within existing **legacy systems** that don't know how to talk to one another. Because many of these tasks are closely related, there is immense duplication of code across applications. Combining related tasks into common objects can eliminate this duplication, producing systems that are smaller, simpler, and easier to change.

Second, you don't have to convert overnight. Depending on the construction of the applications you are using today, much of the actual "grunt work" assigned to an object can be delegated to an existing application. A *Product* object wouldn't include all the functionality of a computer-aided design (CAD) application, nor would it control the production of that product on the factory floor. Instead, it would invoke existing applications as required to modify a design or initiate a production run. In essence, the *Product* object would act as a central coordinator for these tasks across the organization, pulling together related information and behavior but not necessarily storing that information or executing that behavior directly.

Existing systems can carry the load

Similarly, a *Customer* object wouldn't actually prepare a customer invoice or send overdue notices; these tasks would be handled by the accounting system. What the *Customer* would do is trigger these events according to policies captured within the object. It would also enforce other policies, such as refusing to permit further sales if the real-world customer is no longer in good standing. In essence, the *Customer* object specializes in coordinating customer interactions, ensuring that all these interactions are in harmony with one another and in accordance with company policy.

Objects specialize in coordination

The ease with which existing applications can be accessed depends on how they are structured. The easiest applications to access have well-defined **application programming interfaces** (**APIs**) that allow their various functions to be invoked independently. In this case, you can use a technique called **wrapping** to make these functions look like objects to your model, allowing the model to get services from them by sending them messages. It's an elegant solution that can greatly extend the useful life of existing systems.

Legacy integration can be easy

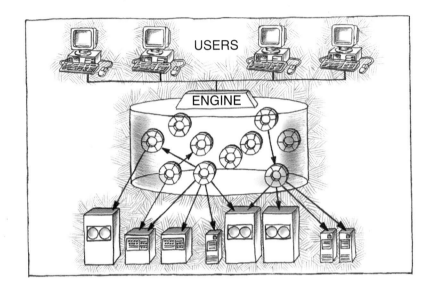

It can also be extremely difficult

The hardest applications to use are those that can't be called by other programs at all. In this case, you have to use special tools, such as **screen scrapers** and **keyboard emulators**, to "fool" the application into thinking that a controlling object is really a person sitting at a terminal performing a task manually. This second option isn't pretty, and it can be thrown off by even the smallest change in the user interface of the existing application. But it often works as an interim strategy until you can replicate the functions of an existing application within your object model.

A New Synthesis

Eventually, object engines will go far beyond the role of application coordinators. This old-but-new technology represents the first opportunity in the history of software to bring about a true synthesis of two major forms of business information—namely, procedures and data. As object engines take their hard-won place in the market, entire business models will be designed, simulated, and executed in a single environment. They are the ultimate replacement for the monolithic applications of old.

Entire companies will execute in engines

The transition from applications to engines won't happen overnight because it, too, is a paradigm shift—the distinction between programs and databases is far too ingrained for systems managers to give it up lightly. But the changeover has already begun, and it will eventually spread to encompass all the mission-critical systems of organizations. At that point, developers will look back and wonder why anyone would ever have wanted to separate procedures and data in the first place!

The change will be slow but lasting

8

Objects for the Enterprise

Object technology has proven its value in numerous projects from small pilots to large-scale, mission-critical systems. The technology is now moving up to the level of the enterprise, where it offers new opportunities for building integrated, adaptive business environments. But tackling the enterprise involves issues of distribution, scalability, and integration that rarely arise in isolated applications. This chapter examines the tools and techniques that allow objects to play—and play well—at the enterprise level.

Distributing Objects

Conveying Messages

The first step in distributing objects is opening up a channel of communications between remote objects. This is done through a technology called an **object request broker** (**ORB**). An ORB acts as a message bus, transporting a message from an object in one location, delivering it to a target object in some other location, and then returning a response to the originating object.

The first challenge is to open a channel

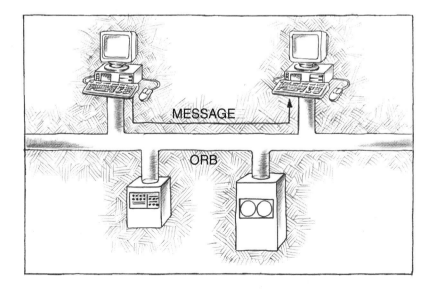

Remote messaging using an ORB

CORBA is the industry-standard ORB	The industry standard for ORBs is the Common Object Request Broker Architecture (CORBA) specified by the Object Management Group (OMG). There are numerous CORBA-compatible ORBs available today from a wide variety of vendors ranging from start-up companies to such industry mainstays as IBM, HP, and Sun. ORBs are in daily use throughout the world and represent a safe, proven technology. The latest incarnation of CORBA, the **Internet Interoperability ORB Protocol** (**IIOP**), bridges ORBs from multiple vendors while adding support for object communications across the **Internet**.
Microsoft and Sun-Soft offer alternatives	The consensus built up by the OMG is strong but falls short of being unanimous. At present, the major holdout is Microsoft, which has a major investment in its own Windows-specific **Distributed Component Object Model** (**DCOM**), an extension of its COM technology. COM and DCOM are now being ported to other platforms, so the Windows-only restriction may soon be lifted. JavaSoft, the Java division of SunSoft, is offering its **Remote Method Invocation** (**RMI**) technology for communications between remote objects written in Java. Like Java itself, RMI is inherently platform-independent. But, being specific to Java, it is not language-independent as are CORBA and DCOM.
The ORB market is wide open	Right now, it isn't clear whether a single protocol will win the ORB wars. There is strong support for CORBA because it represents an industry standard agreed upon by more than 700 companies rather than a technology promoted by a single vendor. But commercial tools are already available to bridge the different offerings, and multiple ORB technologies can probably coexist without harming the object marketplace.

Masking Location

The next step up in distributing objects is **location transparency**, which relieves objects of the burden of tracking the location of all the objects they send messages to. Each of the three messaging systems provides some form of object location service, which may be based on either names or numeric identifiers. In each case, the mechanics are the same: The sender of a message first asks the location service for the location of the receiver and then sends the message to that location.

Location transparency is essential

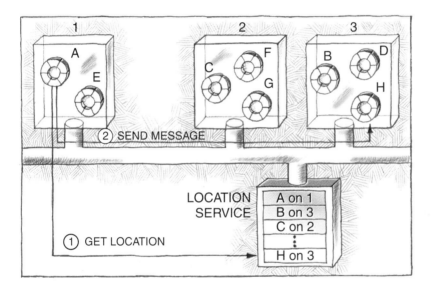

Using a location service

A further step up on the distribution scale is **remoteness transparency**, which hides the very fact that an object is located on a different machine. The most common mechanism for achieving this result is the use of **proxy objects**. A proxy is a local representative of an object that is located on a remote machine. The proxy presents the object's interface to other objects on the local machine, appearing to them as a local object. Behind the shield of its encapsulation, it forwards all requests for services to the real object

Remoteness transparency is better

on the remote machine. When the real object has responded to the message, the proxy receives the real object's response and passes it back to the original requestor. An object can distribute as many proxies as it needs to ensure that it appears to be local to any object that talks to it.

Messaging through a proxy object

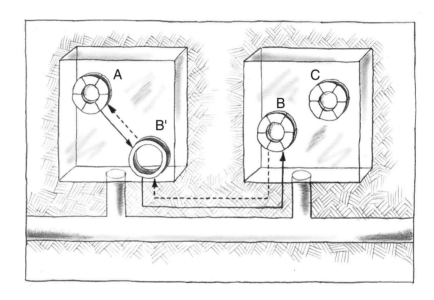

Proxies can talk to other proxies

The beauty of proxy objects is that they eliminate the need to know that the target of a message is remote, look up its location, and engage the services of an ORB to send the message. Objects just send messages to one another in the same execution space. If the receiver happens to be located on another machine, a proxy object hides that fact and handles the remote communications automatically. When you consider that many of the other objects on a given machine may themselves be proxies for objects on still other machines, the power of this approach quickly becomes apparent. Through the use of proxies, objects distributed across any number of machines can function as one virtual system without regard to location.

Proxies offer another advantage: They allow objects to be moved without affecting any of the systems that contain either the original object or its proxies. This is possible because a proxy is interchangeable with the original—the interface is identical, and encapsulation ensures that there is no way any other object can know which is real and which is a proxy. The only operational difference is that proxies don't respond as quickly because of the delay in relaying messages and returning responses over an ORB. The goal, then, is to place the original object where it has the most frequent interactions with other objects, leaving proxies to handle locations that get less message traffic.

Proxies allow objects to be moved

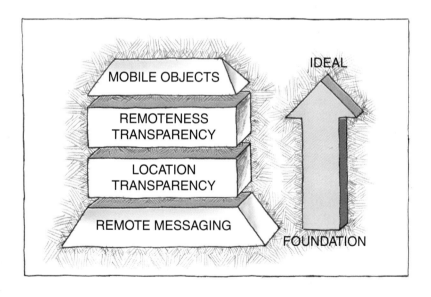

Levels of support for distribution

Mobile Objects

The ideal solution for distributed object systems is to allow objects to move themselves freely from machine to machine within a virtual object space. This capability is just starting to become a commercial reality. Java offers the ability to define objects that can move themselves over a network today, and it appears likely that other object environments will attempt to add this mobility in the near future.

Mobile objects are the best solution

Mobile objects support load balancing	Mobile objects allow **dynamic load balancing**, in which objects automatically seek out computers with free cycles. This capability has been a long-sought goal because it will allow companies to use their machines more effectively. It is not uncommon for a company to be running a small number of mission-critical machines at full capacity, yet be tapping no more than 10 to 15 percent of its total computing capability. If idle desktop and departmental machines could be used to dynamically off-load some of the computing tasks, many companies could multiply their peak computing capacity by a factor of 4 or 5 without buying additional hardware.
Network bandwidth can also be conserved	Mobile objects can also help conserve network bandwidth. If an object finds that it is spending most of its time interacting with objects on a different machine, it can relocate itself to that machine for the duration of the interactions. This ability will be especially important as object systems scale up to the global level, particularly as more companies begin to use the Internet for distributed computing.
Mobile objects permit flexible architectures	Finally, mobile objects provide the foundation for more flexible computing architectures. A great deal of energy is currently being devoted to figuring out the "best" architecture for distributed computing, with the client-server model giving way to the three-tier model, which is now losing ground to a five-tier model. Although some layering may be desirable in a network architecture, it is important not to sacrifice too much flexibility. Mobile objects can operate within a tiered architecture, but they are more effective in an open architecture in which each machine can play a different role depending on the objects it is executing at any given moment.

From Objects to Agents

The Need for Rules

It is an unfortunate fact that most objects are rather stupid. They contain methods for executing procedures, and they have variables to hold the inputs and outputs of those procedures. But they lack a good mechanism for capturing the rules that determine when and how these procedures should be carried out. If you ask them to do something, they do it. If you don't, they just sit there. In business terms, objects understand procedures but are clueless when it comes to policies.

Objects aren't very intelligent

This is not to say that objects can't contain decision logic that influences the execution of their procedures. But, given that objects are comprised entirely of methods and variables, that logic has to be encoded within methods. This is unfortunate because it means that business policies must be "hard-coded" into objects. If a policy is changed, programmers must be called in to reprogram any affected objects, the modified system must be retested to make sure it still works properly, and then the system must be redeployed on all the machines that use it. Embedding policies in program code makes objects rigid and hard to modify, a practice that undermines the goal of adaptive systems.

Policies can be programmed into methods

I suspect that the only reason businesses put up with this situation is that it is just an object-oriented variant on the way software has always been developed. For 50 years, business policies have been hard-coded into procedures. For 50 years, companies have been unable to change their policies quickly because it took too long to reprogram these systems. In some cases, the original policies have been lost altogether, leaving programs as the sole repository of knowledge about the policies it implements. More than one company has found itself wading through millions of lines of COBOL code to figure out how it actually conducts its business!

This is standard practice in business

*Objects need a third
kind of ingredient*

In making the move to objects, our industry has simply combined
the two primary ingredients of software: procedures and data. Although bringing these two together has many benefits, it doesn't
offer any more flexibility with regard to representing policies. Fortunately, it is relatively easy to solve this problem. We just have to
add a third kind of ingredient to objects: rules. If we expand the
definition of objects to consist of methods, variables, and rules, we
have everything we need to make objects intelligent and adaptive.

*Rules are just a third
kind of information*

At the logical level, adding rules to objects is only a modest extension, and it's fully in keeping with the principles of object technology. Recall that an object encapsulates everything it needs to know
in order to act on behalf of its corresponding real-world object. As
described earlier, data and procedures are just two different kinds
of information, corresponding to the "what" and the "how" of an
object. Rules simply add a third kind of information, addressing the
"when" and the "whether" questions, which allows objects to use a
bit more discretion in deciding what to do under different conditions.

**A third kind of
information**

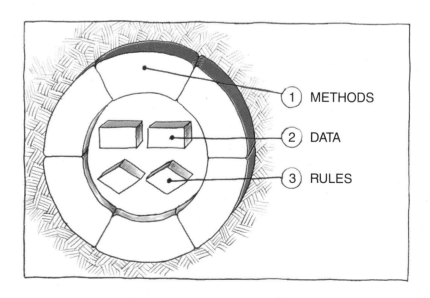

Building in Rules

Regardless of how your enterprise design is to be implemented, you should assume discrete, modifiable business rules as a key design element. This allows you to make each object as generic and flexible as possible because any behavior that is situation-specific can be handled by a rule. For example, designing discount policies into the methods of a product object is a sure way to shorten the useful life of that object. Instead, design the methods to call on discounting rules and then specify the rules separately. This approach yields two benefits: The rules remain visible to managers, and they are more easily changed in response to business demands.

Design your business around rules

Another important practice is to fully encapsulate rules within objects. There are object development systems on the market that provide excellent support for rules but that define the rules outside the objects and allow them to control objects rather than tucking the rules inside the objects. Such tools tend to cripple the autonomy of objects while encouraging the construction of large, monolithic rule bases. Rule bases of this kind are expensive to build and hard to maintain. It is also quite difficult to integrate the knowledge of multiple human experts because different experts tend to create conflicting rules.

Don't build separate rule bases

Placing rules outside of objects

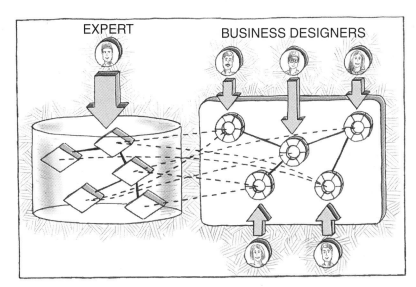

EXPERT   BUSINESS DESIGNERS

Encapsulate rules within objects

Designing rules into each object and hiding them behind the object's message interface restores the autonomy of objects. This practice also allows rules to be modified locally without creating global side effects, and it facilitates the integration of knowledge from many human experts. For example, people from sales and marketing can define discounting rules, and people within manufacturing can define rules for allocating operators to shifts. These rules can be defined and refined at different times without affecting a running business model except to improve its performance. There is no loss of analytical power to this encapsulation because there is no reason for such rules to even know of one another's existence, much less interact with each other directly.

Placing rules within objects

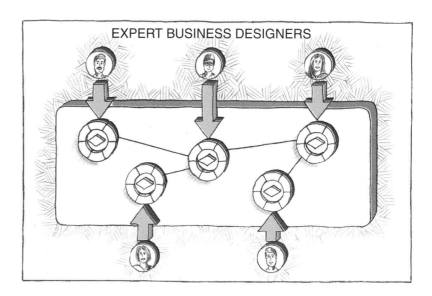

Implement rules as separate objects

How you actually implement the rules you design depends strongly on your chosen development environment. If you work with a system that allows rules to be defined as part of object definition, you already have the tools you need. If not, it is a good idea to define rules as separate objects that are invoked from object methods. This allows the rules to be defined and maintained separately from the methods and variables, carrying the visibility and modifiability established during design into implementation.

Rules can be supported by defining a single *Rule* class. In its simplest form, this class has two components:

Rule objects can be quite simple

1. A *condition*, which is a variable or method that evaluates to true or false
2. An *action*, which is a method defined within the class that contains the rule

Whenever you send a rule object an execute message, it checks to see whether its condition is true. If it is, it executes its action. Otherwise, it does nothing. It is helpful to give these rule objects names that reflect their logic to make them more self-evident.

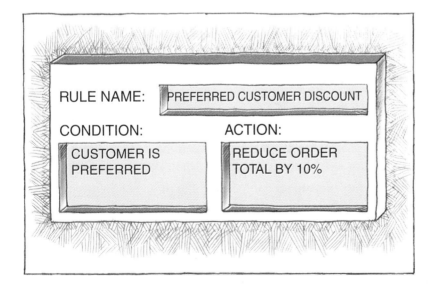

A sales order discount rule

RULE NAME: PREFERRED CUSTOMER DISCOUNT

CONDITION: ACTION:

CUSTOMER IS PREFERRED   REDUCE ORDER TOTAL BY 10%

Many variations are possible

Once you have an initial *Rule* class working, you can easily go on to add variations, possibly as subclasses. For example, it is convenient to have a rule type that includes an *alternative action* term that triggers a different action when the condition is false. It is also a good idea to allow either or both of the action terms to contain other rules, allowing rules to be nested to handle more complex business decisions.

Nested rules determining a discount

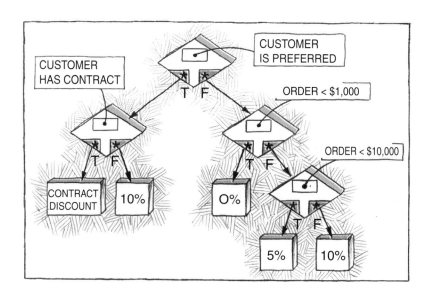

Composite rules are also useful

Another useful form is a composite rule that contains a list of component rules. These component rules can be combined in a variety of different ways. For example, you can list the rules according to priority and execute each one in turn, until one of them carries out an action or the end of the list is reached. Alternatively, you can execute all the rules and take as many actions as are called for. Yet another variant is to allow composite rules to include other composite rules, allowing highly flexible sets of rules to be defined. The kinds of rules required by your design will dictate the types of *Rule* classes you need to define.

The ideal is to implement rules in a way that allows them to be changed without reprogramming. Preferably, it should be possible for managers to change these rules directly and immediately, without having to call on technical personnel for assistance. Failing that, adding a rule should be something that can be done very quickly on an ad hoc basis. As a practical guideline, it is relatively easy to define composite rules dynamically because all these objects do is manage lists of other rules. Basic rules are more challenging because they call methods and send messages, which typically requires some reprogramming. However, it is possible with a bit of effort to build rule classes that perform automatic code generation. This is greatly facilitated by the use of dynamic languages such as Smalltalk and Java.

Make rules as dynamic as possible

Objects as Agents

If objects are mobile and use rules to guide their actions, they can take on a great deal of responsibility within a business system. In effect, every object becomes an active agent representing and guiding the actions of its corresponding real-world object. Agent objects can monitor your information systems and watch for changes, scan the Internet for useful information, carry out routine business transactions while you sleep, and perform many other useful tasks.

Objects are morphing into agents

This idea of objects as agents requires a bit of industry context. Agent technology is the new software buzzword, with many parties claiming and clamoring for agents. This takes a little pressure off object technology to be the solution to every problem on the planet, but it also makes it sound as though we had moved on to something new and different. Agent technology *can* be viewed as an alternative to object technology, but it is much more effective to implement it as an *extension* to objects. In my view, agents are nothing more or less than objects with rules and legs.

Agents are objects with rules and legs

Designing for Scalability

Enterprise systems must scale well

As every large company knows, size is the enemy of adaptivity. The larger a system grows, the more interdependent its pieces become and the harder it is to change any part without breaking the whole. The best way to ward off this rigidity is to design flexibility into a system right from the outset and then ensure that each incremental expansion respects and maintains that flexibility. This book describes a number of techniques that will help you achieve this goal. The following four sections of this chapter summarize these techniques in the form of four "laws" of object design. Following these guidelines won't guarantee success, but it will definitely help you instill adaptivity into your systems and retain that adaptivity as your systems expand across the enterprise.

1. Never Model an Object Outside of Itself

The first law preserves object integrity

In my experience, the most important rule of object design is never to model an object outside of itself. This rule keeps your model as simple as possible, and it offers a single point of change when you need to make modifications. It also eliminates redundancies that waste resources and can cause costly errors.

Example: a Customer object

If you have a *Customer* object, then use that object to handle all your interactions with the real-world customer and also to contain all information and rules pertaining to that customer. Don't allow the sales, service, and manufacturing organizations to design their own variations on the *Customer* object, even though they may each do something slightly different with customers. Allowing this proliferation of overlapping objects will soon lead to duplicate and conflicting customer information at both the procedure level and the data level. It will also fractionate operations that should be bound together, making it difficult to coordinate your interactions with a customer. Finally, it is much harder to add, remove, or modify customer objects when they occur in different forms and locations.

As an added bonus, the first law also makes inheritance more effective. If you define subclasses of the *Customer* class, you can be assured that they will inherit all the qualities of customers and function properly throughout the organization. If business knowledge about customers is spread across multiple classes, each of these classes could require subclassing in order to achieve the desired specialization. Coordinating multiple, related class hierarchies greatly complicates the use of inheritance and invites errors in both design and execution.

Effective inheritance is ensured

2. Specify Objects by Their Interfaces

The second law of object design is to specify objects by their interfaces rather than their classes. Following this rule helps you build classes that can be used independently of one another, allowing class libraries to function like real-world libraries. It also facilitates combining classes built in different parts of your organization or purchased from different vendors. In addition, it allows more flexibility within a business design because objects constrained by interfaces don't have to come from the same branch of the class hierarchy.

The second law increases pluggability

At the same time, following this law increases security because you can restrict interactions between two objects to a single component interface rather than giving them access to the full capabilities of an object. Finally, using interfaces simplifies object distribution because objects don't have to know about classes defined on other machines. Message interfaces tell them everything they need to know in order to communicate with remote objects.

Security and distribution are enhanced

Example: a distribution system

In a distribution system, a product shipment may have to pass through many different kinds of physical locations, including loading docks, warehouses, inspection stations, and distribution companies. It would be ill advised to design a class hierarchy in which all these entities were subclasses of physical location—they all share the property of *having* a location, but they aren't *special cases* of a location. Constraining these distribution points using a location interface rather than a *Location* class allows any conceivable mix of objects that have locations. The *Shipment* is allowed to access only location information with these distribution points, preventing it from interacting in ways beyond its business scope. Finally, the *Shipment* can talk to distribution points anywhere in the world without having to know about the classes defined at these remote locations.

3. Make Objects Independent Agents

The third law empowers objects to act

Some books on object design advocate the use of "managed objects." To me, the phrase is an oxymoron. A well-designed object can manage itself just fine, thank you very much, and attempts to control it from the outside may well destroy its usefulness in a large-scale business system. The managed-object approach reduces modifiability because changing the capabilities of an object requires altering both the object itself and any objects that are responsible for managing it. Also, empowered objects, like empowered people, tend to get work done with a minimum of fuss and cross talk.

Example: managing shipments

A good illustration of a managed object is the *Shipment* object mentioned in the preceding example. In the normal course of distribution management, a shipment would be planned from the top down, and each of its movements would be as tightly controlled as possible. This is considered the normal and necessary procedure in business for managing the complexity of shipments, particularly where multiple shipments may share transportation and must be coordinated. Yet, as Chapter 9 demonstrates, an effective way to optimize a distribution network is to allow every shipment to fend for itself, seeking its own path to its destination and "sharing rides" with other shipments where their paths coincide. In this case, unmanaged shipments acting as independent agents may offer a better solution to the business problem while eliminating much of the administrative overhead of managing the distribution process.

4. Encapsulate Objects in Nested Nines

The final law states that objects should be used to encapsulate other objects on multiple levels with no more than nine objects at each level. The goal here is to make large-scale designs as simple and well-structured as possible. Research has shown that the span of mental apprehension is about five to nine discrete items. A "flat" design consisting of 729 objects—not a particularly large number in software designs—is nearly impossible for people to grasp. In this design, there are more than half a million potential connections to consider! However, the same design structured in three levels of nested nines can be understood without considering more than 81 potential connections—and usually far fewer—at any one time.

The fourth law gives structure to designs

The rule of nested nines

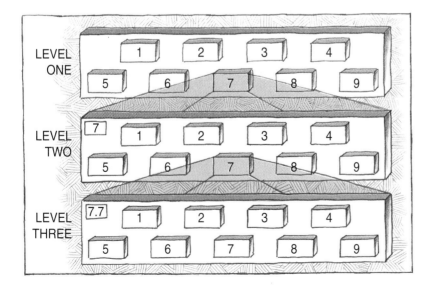

Good encapsulation is essential	This simplification only works if the encapsulation is sound. If components in one object have direct access to the components of other objects, encapsulation is broken, and the design no longer has independent levels. But if encapsulation is maintained, the design is not only mentally manageable but also highly modifiable because any object at any level can be restructured without affecting the others. This leads to very flexible designs whose components can evolve independently over time without disturbing the design as a whole. The organic analog of this technique is the three-level modularization of cells, organs, and systems seen in the human body, as described in Chapter 2.
Example: organizations as objects	The trick to using this technique, of course, is to find the right high-level objects. In enterprise-level designs, these objects are almost always organizations. In fact, company org charts quite often reflect the law of nested nines, perhaps in unconscious recognition of our limited span of apprehension. Using objects to represent the organizations of a company and bring together the processes and resources managed by each organization is a natural reflection of both good design and business realities.
Objects strengthen organizational autonomy	Respecting organizational boundaries is considerably easier with the support of an object system. Sending written requests up and down the hierarchy of an organization can be expensive and time-consuming, leading people to cut across organizational boundaries in order to reduce time and costs. But they do so at the greater cost of breaking the autonomy of organizations, limiting the ability of each to evolve better ways of providing the requested services. With object messaging, the overhead of respecting organizational boundaries is measured in pennies and hundredths of a second. Designing object-based workflow that honors these boundaries has a very high benefit-to-cost ratio.

9

The Adaptive Organization

The central theme of this book is that object technology is an ideal foundation for building adaptive business systems. Designing scalable, executable models that span the enterprise, as described in the preceding chapters, is critical to realizing the goal of adaptive systems. But it isn't sufficient. Adaptivity is an elusive property—it is everywhere you look in natural systems, but it's hard to capture in business systems. This final chapter offers some insights into the nature of adaptivity and suggests ways to use objects to instill it in your own organization. The closing section of the chapter provides three concrete illustrations of how objects can support the goal of adaptivity.

Understanding Adaptive Systems

Characteristics of Adaptive Systems

One of the most exciting new areas of scientific research is the study of **complex adaptive systems**. Examples include everything from the collective behavior of ants to the evolution of life itself. The common quest in studying these phenomena is to understand how complex order can arise out of the interaction of relatively simple components. How did life emerge out of the interaction of inert molecules? How do termites cooperate to build arches and other architectural structures? How do the phenomena of thought and consciousness arise out of the interaction of neurons in the brain?

Complex adaptive systems create order

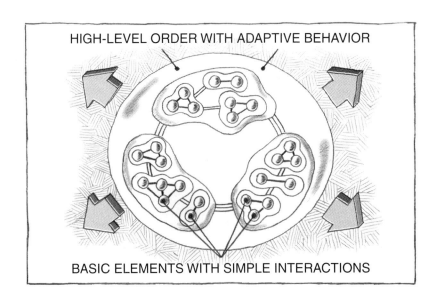

HIGH-LEVEL ORDER WITH ADAPTIVE BEHAVIOR

BASIC ELEMENTS WITH SIMPLE INTERACTIONS

Adaptive systems have common properties

The study of complex adaptive systems is new, but some common properties of these systems have already been identified. Here are five of the most prominent characteristics:

They are grown, not built

1. Complex adaptive systems are never engineered from scratch. Rather, they evolve out of simpler forms through natural selection, increasing their complexity in response to competitive pressures to survive.

They are highly decentralized

2. Adaptive systems work from the bottom up. Despite our persistent attempts to discover them, there are no centralized controls to coordinate behavior. The exquisite synchronization of birds in flight results from a few simple rules that are followed by every bird in a flock; the notion of a lead bird is a scientific myth.

They tolerate and learn from errors

3. Adaptive systems are highly redundant, with collective behavior emerging from the interaction of a great many components. These systems not only survive errors, they thrive on them. If a local aberration offers improved performance, it quickly spreads throughout the system.

4. Adaptive systems tend to hover right on the edge of control, being easily nudged out of equilibrium but quickly righting themselves after a disruption. Some nudges push them into a new and more adaptive state, which is how they evolve as a whole.

They maintain dynamic equilibrium

5. Adaptive systems exhibit emergent properties—characteristics that are not found in their elements. An example of an emergent property is the wetness that appears when two gases, hydrogen and oxygen, are combined to form water. More interesting examples are the emergence of life out of molecular interactions and the emergence of consciousness out of the interactions of neurons.

They exhibit emergent properties

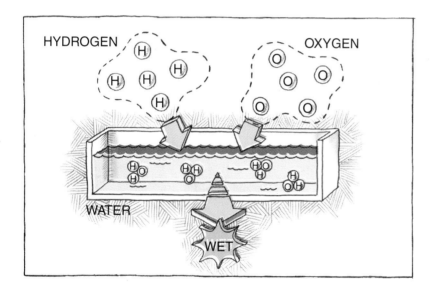

Wetness as an emergent property

Organizations as Adaptive Systems

*Organizations are
adaptive systems*

Organizations qualify as complex adaptive systems and are now being studied in this context. Moreover, the markets in which organizations compete are also adaptive systems. In the spirit of the questions raised earlier, one could just as easily ask the following: How can organizations create immensely complex physical systems, such as commercial aircraft, that are far beyond the capabilities of individual minds? How can free markets, using only a single parameter (price), manage to balance the incredibly complex economics of global supply and demand?

*Organizations are a
unique hybrid*

Understanding adaptivity in organizations represents a unique challenge because an organization is a combination of organic and engineered components. At their core, organizations are groups of people working together to perform actions that are beyond the capabilities of a single individual. But simply huddling a few thousand people together does not an organization make. Getting thousands of people to exhibit coordinated behavior requires shared objectives, common values, defined roles, structured relationships, consistent policies and a variety of other social inventions. It also requires a physical infrastructure including buildings, machines, tools, supplies, communication media, and a host of other human artifacts designed for the purpose.

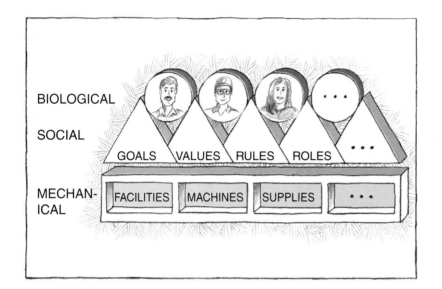

BIOLOGICAL

SOCIAL

GOALS VALUES RULES ROLES

MECHAN-
ICAL FACILITIES MACHINES SUPPLIES • • •

All these ingredients must be properly mixed and allocated in order for an organization to function in an adaptive way. Ultimately, however, the driving force toward adaptivity comes from the organic component of organizations—namely, their people. But the emphasis is on the plural, not the singular. The seeds of adaptivity may be found in the actions of individuals, but no organization can survive for long if individual actions do not combine in a way that supports the adaptation of the organization as a whole. Increasing the adaptivity of a large organization requires enhancing communication among its members and aligning their actions toward a common goal.

Adaptivity is driven by people

We must embrace organic qualities

Viewing organizations as complex adaptive systems is neither widespread nor well received among senior managers today. This is hardly surprising given that the view is antithetical to most contemporary attempts to improve organizations. Business engineering is very much in vogue; top-down control is still the rule in most organizations; errors are regarded as events to be eliminated rather than learned from; and stable structures are an abiding goal. Eventually, however, we must learn to embrace and encourage the organic qualities of organizations because these are the wellspring of adaptivity. For those who want to explore this frontier ahead of the pack, the following section provides some guidance.

Increasing Organizational Adaptivity

Degrees of Adaptivity

There are degrees of adaptivity

Adaptivity is a matter of degree, not an all-or-none property that an organization either has or doesn't have. In thinking about adaptivity, it is useful to distinguish among three different levels—namely, reactivity, proactivity, and creativity:

Reactivity follows the market

1. The reactive organization tracks changes in the market and tries to adapt to them as quickly as possible. The shorter the reaction time, the more competitive the organization. But no matter how fast the reactive organization adapts, it always lags behind the market.

Proactivity tracks the market

2. The proactive organization uses historical trends to anticipate changes in the market. Its goal is to make its adjustments in advance of market shifts so that it is perfectly adapted to the market at all times. Because it predicts market changes before they happen, it has more time to make its internal changes and be ready for each change. This is a major competitive advantage over the reactive organization.

3. The creative organization doesn't react to or predict change; it *creates* change. It can do this in a variety of ways: Introducing fundamentally new products, inventing new pricing structures, producing quantum jumps in quality, and defining new market segments are just a few of the available techniques. Because it *defines* the market, the creative organization doesn't need to follow or predict changes in the market.

Creativity defines the market

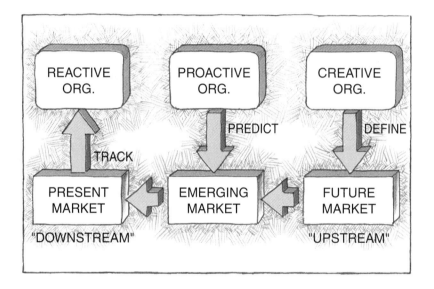

To see the power of reaching the third level, you need only compare ourselves to the other species with whom we share this planet. All living things are able to react to change, some are able to anticipate change, but only humans *create* change on a global scale. For better or for worse, our actions now define the environment within which all other species must struggle to survive.

Human beings epitomize creativity

Clearly, the best place for a company to be is in the third category, continuously redefining the market and keeping the competition perpetually off balance. IBM once enjoyed this position in the computer industry. There was a deep truth in the old expression that IBM wasn't the competition, it was the environment. Today, Microsoft enjoys a similar position. But the evolution of the Internet and the spark of creativity known as Java have radically altered the computing environment, and Microsoft is even now creatively reinventing itself to retain its position of dominance. And so it continues.

Achieving Adaptability

The first step toward increased adaptability is a simple yet profound change in perspective. It is important to view your organization as a living system, not an engineered machine. Living systems evolve through incremental changes that confer increased competitiveness in their environment. Unlike machines, they are not centrally controlled and regimented into perfect execution. To embrace this new perspective, you must be willing to let go of the desire for increased control and begin to encourage the variability and experimentation that are essential to adaptive change.

Encouraging variability and experimentation necessarily means giving more autonomy to line organizations and individuals. But simply surrendering control is hardly the answer—that way lies chaos, not competitiveness. The key to decentralizing control while maintaining organizational adaptivity is to provide clear feedback on the fitness of individual initiatives. If a person or group behaves in a way that increases the fitness of the organization as a whole, that person or group should be rewarded with increased funding and opportunities for growth within the organization. In this way, the mechanism of natural selection is encouraged to work *within* organizations as well as between organizations.

One technique for achieving this feedback is to introduce free-market economics within an organization. This requires establishing redundant groups providing comparable services and allowing them to compete for business within the organization. This redundancy may introduce some inefficiencies, but these are offset by the improvements that smaller groups and local initiative can produce. This approach also employs a proven metric for fitness feedback—namely, profitability. Groups that offer better services at lower cost will thrive and grow at the expense of less competitive providers. These improvements, in turn, enhance the fitness of the organization as a whole, ensuring that local optimization is in line with global optimization.

Leverage free-market economics

The use of internal competition is not, of course, a new idea—it has been practiced successfully for years within a number of major organizations. What is remarkable is that it is still *viewed* as a new idea. The wholesale adoption of free-market economies around the world over the last ten years, including the dramatic collapse of the Soviet Union, is a powerful demonstration of the superiority of decentralized systems in coping with change. Yet the majority of large corporations are still run as controlled economies. Something is definitely wrong with this picture.

Internal competition is a proven technique

Some of the resistance to internalizing market economics may be a reluctance to unleash the cutthroat quality of survival of the fittest within organizations. But natural selection can be tempered with a human touch. In one variant of this approach, sometimes called "coopetition," practices developed by superior groups are periodically shared with other groups and spread throughout the organization. Even if groups that can't compete fall by the wayside, internal "outplacement" can still assure that the careers and livelihoods of effective employees are protected.

Natural selection can be humane

Encourage variability and tolerate errors

An organization that improves through variation must have a high tolerance for errors. This can be achieved through redundant groups, as previously described, and through redundant quality checks throughout a company's value-adding operations. The goal is to allow new ideas to prove themselves while sheltering customers from the effects of ideas that don't work out. This approach is quite different from a zero-defects approach to managing operations. A company with no tolerance for errors at the operational level runs the risk of discovering that it has no capacity for adaptivity. If you can devise a system that tolerates variation from fixed policies in search of improvement, yet provides quick containment of variations that could cause harm, you have the right mix for rapid evolution.

Strive for dynamic equilibrium

The ability to maintain dynamic equilibrium is essential for an organization that is thriving on change. This means that you must achieve balance through motion rather than using the status quo as your source of stability. It's like the difference between sitting and walking. Walking is a dynamic process of falling forward, catching yourself, falling forward again, and so on. In humans, walking is a learned skill, and a child experiences a giddy sense of power when he or she first learns to stay in balance while moving forward at this exhilarating pace. So it is with organizations. In a business environment that demands constant change, organizations must learn to maintain their balance while moving forward at ever-increasing speeds. Once the initial fear is overcome, it can be a heady experience.

One final suggestion is to be on the alert for new and interesting phenomena within the organization. If a group collaboration tool leads to a new level of problem solving that couldn't have been achieved through conventional meetings, that is an emergent property that should be recognized and harnessed for the good of the organization. If large numbers of objects operating as independent agents begin pulling the company in a different direction, that, too, is an emergent property that should be studied and exploited. Expecting, exploring, and expanding on new and surprising behaviors within the organization is an important step toward adaptivity. It is also the step that is most likely to propel the organization into the third level of adaptivity—namely, creativity.

Nurture emergent properties

Adaptivity Through Objects

Objects are naturally adaptive elements. If allowed to interact freely, managing their own actions, they can be excellent components for building up adaptive systems. The trick is to give them enough structure that they can be channeled in the right direction, yet leave them enough freedom that their natural adaptivity can produce benefits at the organizational level. In many cases, this requires giving up the cherished illusion of control and allowing objects to coordinate the actions of an organization in an organic, bottom-up manner.

Objects are naturally adaptive

Here are three examples of adaptivity

Here are three simple examples that illustrate how objects can be used to enhance organizational adaptivity. The examples are based on my experiences as a business designer. They are intentionally conservative in that they reflect what is happening in the real world right now, and they only hint at the power of objects to foster adaptivity. The examples are also somewhat generic to protect client-specific designs. But if you fill in the details as they might apply in your own business, then project the ideas forward to a future in which objects are the defining elements of your company, you will soon understand how objects can provide the essential foundation for the adaptive organization.

The 18-Minute Product

New products gestate like elephants

I have often begun design engagements by asking clients how long it takes them to prepare new products for market introduction. The answer is curiously consistent: "About 18 months." I have never found a common cause for this answer, and I'm sure it's just a coincidence that it's the same as the gestation period of an elephant. Whatever the source of the commonality, there is a clear consensus that 18 months is too long, and many companies have goals to reduce this time to a half or a third of its current value.

Why not an 18-minute product?

As one of my client-readiness checks, I sometimes ask whether the company would be interested in collapsing the time down to something more like 18 *minutes*. If the client passes this litmus test—that is, if they don't turn blue when I immerse them in the concept— the rules of engagement have just been changed from making incremental improvements to becoming an adaptive organization. Here is how objects can help make such radically short lead times possible.

Consider telecommunications as an example. It's hard to open the newspaper these days without seeing a full-page ad for a new long-distance dialing program. It may look as though these programs are being defined on the fly as competitive responses to one another, but they have actually been in the works for many months before they are announced. Even if it takes only 18 minutes to think up a new dialing plan, it still takes about 18 months to extend the company's information infrastructure to handle the new plan.

Example: Long-distance dialing plans

The problem here is twofold: Existing applications weren't designed for rapid change, and a great many applications must be altered to support a new product. An object execution system can help with both problems. These systems are designed for sustained evolution, and their components are designed to offer single points of change.

Object systems support rapid change

An object-based telecom business system would certainly contain a class to represent long-distance dialing plans. Let's call this class *DialingPlan*. The *DialingPlan* would be responsible for pricing calls, calculating discounts, generating statements, and coordinating all the essential tasks of administering a long-distance plan. More precisely, it would define the *interfaces* for performing these tasks. Its subclasses, which represent the individual plans, would define how each of these tasks was implemented. For example, a subclass called *UniRate* could simply charge a fixed rate per minute regardless of the physical distance spanned by a call. To introduce a volume-based variant of this plan, we could declare a subclass of *UniRate* that reduced the per-minute charge by 10 percent if the number of minutes used under the plan during the preceding month exceeded some threshold. Defining this new plan would probably require no more than 20 lines of programming code.

Defining products by specialization is fast

Defining a product using subclassing

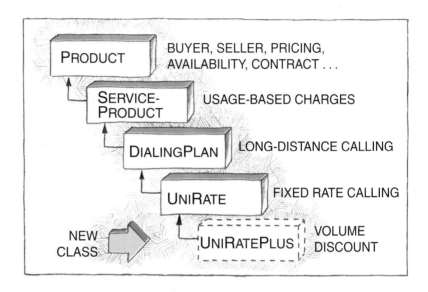

Defining products by composition is faster

An even faster way to define new products is to use composition. Suppose we wanted to introduce a simplified, comprehensive package for small businesses. This package, which we'll call Business First, is defined as a new combination of existing products, including a dialing plan, calling cards, voice messaging, and dial-up Internet access. The company already has a generic *ServiceProduct* class that knows how to charge for itself based on usage and to add in the charges for any other instances of *ServiceProduct* it may contain. To define our new product using composition, we create a *BusinessFirst* object as an instance of *ServiceProduct* and list all the services in the package as its components. Without changing a single line of code, we have a new product ready for sale.

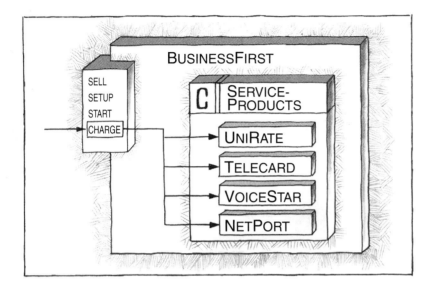

The key to making the 18-minute product work is having a business system in place that uses a common, generic interface for dealing with product objects. As long as a new type of product conforms to this interface, all the supporting systems will absorb it without modification. For example, no alterations are required to add the product to the electronic catalog or to support it in the sales process. The catalog object already knows how to list products, and sales objects already know how to sell them. The new product just glides through these systems as though it had always been there.

The rest of the system absorbs these products

151

Self-Monitoring Loans

The problem is loan delinquencies

The second example illustrates the value of allowing objects to manage themselves rather than attempting to control them. The setting is a national lending company with ten million loans outstanding. The goal is to detect loans that are likely to become delinquent and intervene while there is still a good chance of salvaging them. The stakes are high. Taking a good loan into collections is an expensive mistake. Failing to take a bad loan into collections is an even more expensive mistake.

The company combines two strategies

Unfortunately, it is logistically impossible to individually review ten million loans every month to decide which ones to assign to collection calls. At present, the company pursues two strategies in parallel. First, it initiates collection calls on loans that are overdue by 30 days or more. Second, it uses statistical techniques to predict which kinds of loans are likely to be at risk and examines as many of these loans as it can. Only a tiny percentage of the at-risk loans are actually reviewed.

Loans should monitor themselves

A more effective approach is to represent loans with objects and to make the *Loan* objects responsible for monitoring themselves, requesting a collection call if they exhibit any combination of danger signals. Each loan is notified of relevant events in the real world so that it can make informed decisions about its risk level. For example, a message is sent to the loan whenever a payment comes in, and messages are sent if there is any change in the credit rating of the holder or in the value of the property pledged as collateral. Whenever the loan receives one of these messages, it updates its information and then checks its rules to see whether it requires a collection call.

The one event this system can't catch is a nonevent—the failure of a check to come in on time. This is handled by the loan placing a request with a *Dispatcher* object to send it a *latePayment* message ten days after its average payment date. If the payment comes in before that date, the loan cancels the *latePayment* call and sets one up for the next month. If the date arrives before the payment does, the loan receives the *latePayment* message and requests a collection call.

Late payments are caught by time

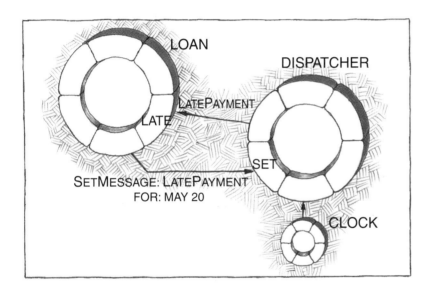

Requesting a latePayment message

Every one of the ten million loans can have a different set of thresholds on its rules. Problem loans can be reigned in by asking the *Dispatcher* object for earlier *latePayment* dates. Loans that have had three or more collection calls can automatically request written notifications. New loans, which carry the highest risk, can watch themselves more carefully than mature loans. Loans can even detect patterns over time that are indicators of increasing risk. If the average payment day is gradually getting later over time, for example, the loan can request a friendly "Is everything okay?" call even if the payments are still within the nominal 30-day grace period.

Each loan has different thresholds

A few rules go a long way

Very little in the way of intelligence is required to make loans appear smart. Collection managers rarely have the luxury of looking at more than five or six pieces of information in deciding whether to send a loan to collections. Simply by checking half a dozen rules in a priority-based sequence, *Loan* objects are able to detect all but a small percentage of the loans that collection managers would single out if they could examine every loan. So, a little bit of intelligence distributed over a large number of independent agents can make the company vastly more intelligent about how it reduces risk in its loans.

The result is much better collections

The result of allowing smart loans to manage themselves is that the lending company now has ten million agents monitoring its loans, each of which is constantly adapting itself to the behavior of a particular loan and striving to minimize its risk. Because each of the loans routinely reports its perceived risk, the company can do a much better job of monitoring its aggregate risk. Moreover, collection managers are freed up to study the results of their self-managing loans and tune the rules to improve performance over time. The bottom line: The company saves money all around, and fewer people wind up losing their homes and cars.

Market-Based Supply Chains

One of the biggest challenges for manufacturing companies is managing the acquisition of goods and materials. The challenge lies in finding a way to ensure sufficient availability to meet projected needs while minimizing inventory expense, transportation costs, spoilage, and a host of other expenses. This problem is referred to as supply chain management because supplies in transit form a chain of movements as they travel from their sources by way of various vehicles, containers, warehouses, distribution points, and other physical locations until they reach their destination. Good supply chain management is essential because even minor mistakes can lead to outages, overages, or other expensive errors.

Manufacturers must manage their supplies

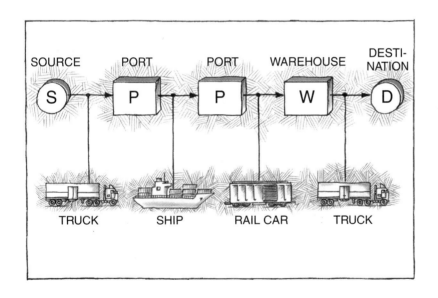

A simple supply chain

Supply chains are very difficult to manage

Managing a single supply chain can be difficult because there are many branch points in the chain, with complex decisions at each point about how to make the next move. Managing multiple supply chains concurrently is even harder because chains overlap at the physical locations, creating opportunities for economies of scale while also placing chains in conflict with one another for scarce resources. When the number of chains becomes large, the problem is nearly impossible to manage effectively. Unfortunately, this situation is the rule rather than the exception: It is not unusual for a manufacturer to manage many thousands of concurrent supply chains.

Overlapping supply chains

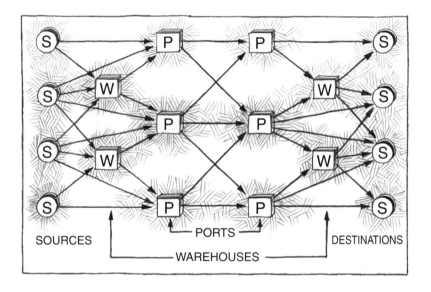

This problem offers an excellent opportunity to apply free-market economics. The core of the model consists of just three classes: *Shipment*, *DistributionPoint*, and *Vehicle*. Shipments know their origin, destination, and any distribution points they are required to pass through along the way, such as customs. Their goal is to arrive at their destination at the required time at the lowest possible cost. Distribution points hold shipments, transfer them to and from vehicles, and request additional vehicles as necessary. Vehicles move shipments from one distribution point to another.

A market model works well here

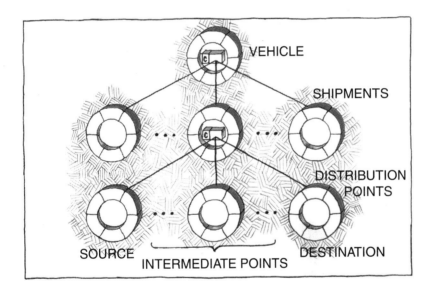

Three classes for supply chains

In this model, there are no fixed chains of distribution. Instead, each shipment is left to find its own way to its destination. To do so, it must pay for storage, loading, transportation, and any other services it needs. It buys these services in open markets that are established at each distribution point. As various shipments converge on a distribution point, they bid against one another for services. The amount they are willing to "pay" depends on their urgency level. These bidding wars are all internal to the object system—the real-world service providers are actually paid the standard rate for handling the shipments that submit the winning bids.

The result of this design is a giant muddle of shipments that are busily planning their routes, bidding against their rivals for services, reserving capacity, and changing their plans when ships don't arrive on time, all the while trying to minimize their total costs. This muddle is, by any reasonable standard, absolutely unmanageable. But it works because it doesn't need management. Instead, it relies on one of the most powerful adaptive systems ever to evolve—the free-market economy. Every element of the economy, including shipments, distribution points, and vehicles, acts in its own best interests. Because they all communicate with one another using a single common parameter—price—the apparent muddle exhibits more order than any top-down control system could ever create.

Appendix: A Software Construction Primer

For more than 50 years, business software has been based on the division between programs, which execute procedures, and databases, which manage data. This practice is in direct conflict to the first principle of object technology, which is to package related procedures and data together. It is essential to understand a half century of thinking before we can appreciate and embrace the radical change that objects will bring to the next 50 years of computing.

The Architecture of Applications

Let's begin by acknowledging a universal truth: Building good software is very, very hard. This is not always obvious to the uninitiated because simple programs are relatively easy to create. The problem lies not in the programming process itself, but in the scaling of this process to systems that span business units, enterprises, and even industries. Not only are these systems hard to construct, they are nearly impossible to change once they are completed. Developing robust, large-scale software systems that can evolve to meet changing needs turns out to be one of the most demanding challenges of modern technology.

Building good software is a major challenge

Applications solve specific problems	With that perspective in mind, let's examine how business software is normally constructed. The standard approach begins with a business problem that can be solved by the application of software—hence, the term "application." The first step in developing an application is to analyze the problem in enough detail to formulate an adequate solution—a process known as requirements analysis. Then, the software is designed, constructed, tested, and deployed—a process that typically takes anywhere from six months to six years.
Applications use programs and databases	The design and construction of an application is based on a fundamental division of labor between software that executes procedures and software that manages data. This division of labor applies not just to the software itself but to the people who design, construct, and manage that software. In most companies that develop software, the group responsible for the company's information systems is, itself, organized around the separation of programming and data management, often with conflicting goals and competing budgets.
The division of labor is well founded	This division of labor, although sometimes extreme in its execution, is based on both solid principles and practical experience in developing business applications. In the early years of software development, each application established and maintained its own data in a form uniquely suited to its needs. This approach optimized individual applications but made it very hard to share data across applications. Over time, data was recognized as an organizational resource that required systematic, standardized management that was independent of the applications that accessed it. This new approach solved the problem of data sharing, and it created a division of labor that helped break down large development projects. The fact that it has also created new problems does not detract from the fact that it has helped make software more manageable for half a century. The following sections explore the techniques used on either side of this division of labor.

Building Programs

The Problem of Scale

A program is nothing more than a series of instructions that tell a computer to carry out specific actions in a particular sequence. Very small programs can be built as a single **procedure**, or sequence of instructions, that performs the desired task. Single-procedure programs are usually written by a single programmer, who can maintain a mental image of the entire procedure, move instructions from place to place, and make design decisions freely as the program unfolds. Small groups of programmers can work in a similar style so long as all the members have free and open communication with one another.

Small programs can be built as a single procedure

Larger programs can't be constructed as a single procedure like this. As the size of a program grows, so does the number of programmers required to build it. When a development group numbers in the tens or hundreds, the amount of communication required among the programmers becomes overwhelming. So many people are negotiating so many interacting decisions that no one has time to do the actual programming!

This approach doesn't work for larger systems

Modular Programming

In principle, the solution to this problem is straightforward: Break large-scale programs down into smaller components that can be constructed independently and then combine them to form the complete system. This general strategy is known as **modular programming**, and it forms the guiding principle behind most of the advances in software construction in the past 40 years.

Larger systems require modular programming

Subroutines support modular programming

The most elementary support for modular programming came with the invention of the **subroutine** in the early 1950s. A subroutine is created by pulling a sequence of instructions out of the main routine and giving it a separate name. Once defined, the subroutine can be executed simply by including its name in the program wherever it is required. Subroutines provide a natural division of labor: Different programmers write the various subroutines and then assemble the completed subroutines into a working program.

Subroutine called from two places

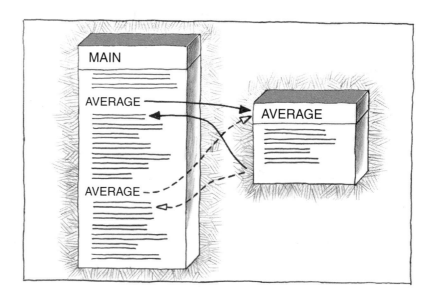

Modular programming requires discipline

While subroutines provide the basic mechanism for modular programming, a lot of discipline is necessary to create well-structured software. Without that discipline, it is all too easy to write torturously complicated programs that are resistant to change, difficult to understand, and nearly impossible to maintain. And that is what happened far too often during the early years of the industry. The solution to this problem was structured programming.

Structured Programming

In the late 1960s, the generally poor state of software sparked a concerted effort among computer scientists to develop a more disciplined, consistent style of programming. The result of that effort was the refinement of modular programming into the approach known as **structured programming**.

Structured programming provides discipline

Structured programming relies on **functional decomposition**, a top-down approach to program design in which a program is systematically broken down into components, each of which is decomposed into subcomponents, and so on, down to the level of individual subroutines. Separate teams of programmers write the various components, which are later assembled into the complete program.

Functional decomposition plays a central role

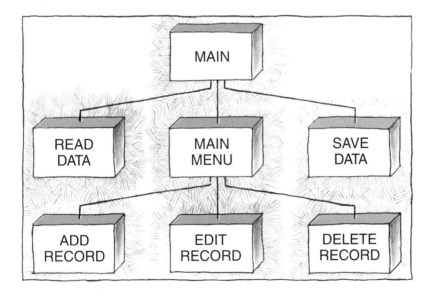

Program with three levels of nesting

Structured programming is useful but limited

Structured programming has produced significant improvements in the quality of software over the last 20 years, but its limitations are now painfully apparent. One of the more serious problems is that it's rarely possible to anticipate the design of a completed system before it's actually implemented. Once the programming is under way, what seemed like a good division of labor at the outset turns out to be the wrong allocation of problems to modules, and the entire design has to be reworked from the top down. The larger the system, the more often this restructuring may take place.

Computer-Aided Software Engineering (CASE)

CASE automates structured programming

A major innovation in structured programming is **computer-aided software engineering** (**CASE**). With CASE, computers manage the process of functional decomposition, graphically defining subroutines in nested diagrams and verifying that all interactions between subroutines follow a correctly specified form. Advanced CASE systems automatically generate the structures for complete programs from these diagrams once all the design information has been entered.

CASE tool building a program

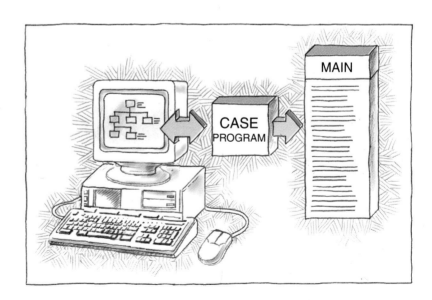

Proponents of CASE heralded the automatic generation of programs from designs as a major breakthrough in software development. However, the process is not nearly as automatic as it first appears. In fact, a CASE tool doesn't create software at all; it simply translates the design for a system from graphical to textual form. Experience has shown that developing a complete graphical design for a program can be just as demanding and time-consuming as writing the program in the first place.

CASE helps, but it doesn't go far enough

Fourth-Generation Languages

Another approach to automatic programming is represented by **fourth-generation languages** (**4GLs**), so called to distinguish them from the conventional "third-generation" languages just discussed. 4GLs include a wide range of tools to help automate the generation of routine business applications, including the creation of forms, reports, and menus.

4GLs can generate programs automatically

4GLs offer many advantages, including the fact that people who are not programmers can use them. The downside of 4GLs is that they can only generate rather simple programs and then only for well-understood problems. Although a programmer can modify these programs by hand to make them more sophisticated, the 4GL can no longer be used to maintain the modified programs. Useful as they are, 4GLs are quickly left behind for all but the simplest applications.

But 4GLs only work for simple, familiar problems

Managing Data

Data must also be modularized

Most efforts to improve software development have focused on the modularization of procedures. But there is another aspect to software that, while less obvious, is no less important. That aspect is the data—the collection of information operated on by the procedures. As the techniques of modular programming have evolved over the years, it has become increasingly apparent that data, too, must be modularized.

Data Within Programs

Subroutines can share small amounts of data

If a program requires only a few pieces of data to perform its tasks, these pieces can safely be made available to all the different subroutines that make up the program. This arrangement is very convenient for programmers because the shared collection of data, typically called **global data**, provides a communal "bulletin board" on which the various subroutines can exchange information whenever they need to communicate.

Shared data with multiple subroutines

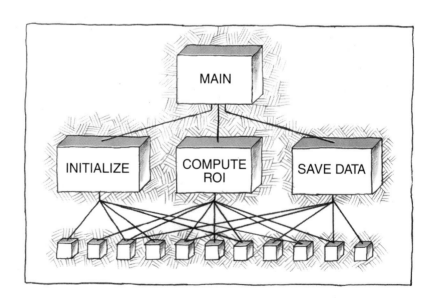

When the pieces of data number in the hundreds or thousands, however, this simple solution usually leads to mysterious errors and unpredictable behavior. The problem is that sharing data is a violation of modular programming, which requires that modules be as independent as possible. Allowing modules to interact freely through shared data makes the actions of any one module dependent on the behavior of all the others. In effect, global data becomes the chink in the armor that structured programming has built around the subroutine.

Sharing too much data leads to problems

The solution to this problem is to modularize the data right along with the procedures. This is typically done by giving each subroutine its own local store of data that it alone can read and write. This strategy of **information hiding** minimizes unwanted interactions between subroutines and allows them to be designed and maintained more independently.

The solution lies in hiding information

Local data within subroutines

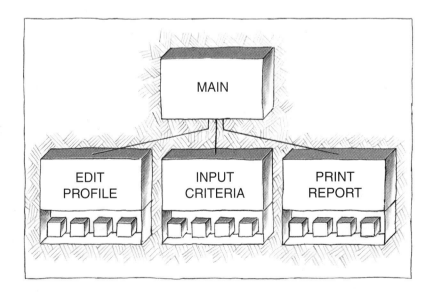

Data Outside of Programs

Some programs don't need to preserve data

Small programs often require only a few inputs and generate output that is meant to be consumed immediately. A program to calculate amortization tables, for example, might accept a base value and an amortization period from the keyboard and then print out a page of calculations. Programs of this sort don't need to store any data because they work with fresh information every time they are run.

But most large programs have to reuse data

Larger programs, however, usually work with the same information over and over again. Inventory control programs, accounting systems, and engineering design tools couldn't function if they didn't have a way of preserving information from one working session to the next.

Data can easily be preserved in files

The simplest solution to the problem of keeping data around is to have a program store its data in an external file. When you finish running the program, it sends the data to the external file. When you start up the program again, it retrieves the data from the file. The use of a file also allows the program to work with more information than it could hold internally by reading and writing only a small portion of the file at any one time.

A program accessing a file

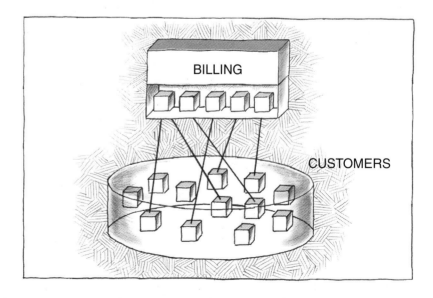

BILLING

CUSTOMERS

External data files provide an adequate solution for information storage so long as the data is only accessed by one user at a time. When data has to be shared across people, programs, or both, new problems arise.

But that doesn't work when data must be shared

Database Management Systems

Most file-based systems will not allow more than one person to access a file at the same time. Allowing different people to access a file simultaneously introduces the possibility of one person changing information that others are currently using. Preventing these confusions turns out to be a fairly difficult technical problem that is not easily solved within simple file-based systems. Although some older programs still use files to store shared information, most multiuser systems are now built on top of special programs, called **database management systems** (**DBMSs**), that are designed to manage simultaneous access to shared data.

Sharing requires a database management system

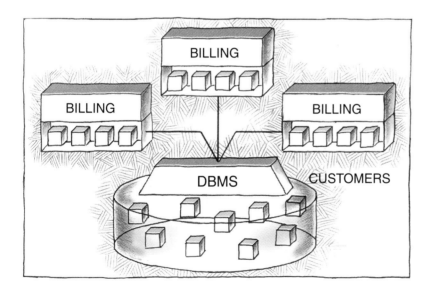

Sharing data in a database

*Early DBMSs fa-
vored navigational
access*

Database management programs do more than just control access
to data stored in files; they also store relationships among the various data elements. The way these relationships are stored is critical
to understanding the generations of databases that have come and
gone in corporate environments. The earliest DBMSs adopted the
approach of storing direct references among data elements, allowing data to be retrieved through a process called **navigational access**. This approach supports extremely fast retrieval of related
information because each piece of stored information includes the
effective locations of all related information.

*The earliest model
was the hierarchic
model*

The earliest form of database manager, known as the **hierarchic
model**, represented data items, called **records**, in tree structures.
For example, a department could include records for the positions
it contained and the equipment checked out to it. Each position, in
turn, could be associated with a list of responsibilities and a list of
employees in the department holding that position.

**Hierarchic database
model**

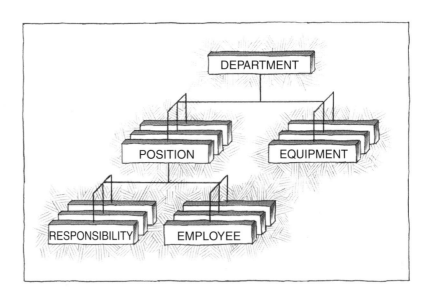

A subsequent extension of the hierarchic model, the **network model**, allowed data to be interconnected freely, with no requirement that it fit into a simple tree structure. In the previous example, each piece of equipment could be associated with both a department and a list of employees who were authorized to use it. This kind of association would not be permitted in the hierarchic model.

The network model extended the hierarchic model

The Rise of the Relational Model

The hierarchic and network database models made it easy to represent complex relationships among data elements and provided fast access to the data. But there was a cost: Accessing the data in a way other than the one supported by the predefined relationships was slow and inefficient. Worse yet, the data structures were hard to modify. Changing these structures required system administrators to shut down the database and rebuild it, modify all the application programs to use the new structures, and then bring all the components of the system back "on line" simultaneously.

Fixed data structures reduce flexibility

The "downtime" created by all these changes was intolerable to users who had to keep working without access to their data or the ability to record their business transactions. Moreover, these changes were highly risky to a company. A single error in any one of the steps just described could easily corrupt the corporate data in a way that could cost a business millions of dollars. The combined effect of these problems was that hierarchic and network databases were very rarely changed once they had been deployed.

This rigidity had serious business consequences

A newer form of database manager, the **relational model**, addresses these problems by removing the information about complex relationships from the database. All data is stored in simple tables, with basic relationships among data items being expressed as references to values in other tables. For example, each entry in an equipment table would contain a value indicating which department it belonged to. This approach to linking data in a DBMS is called **associative access** because it relies on content rather than locations to link data elements together. Along with a new model for accessing data, the relational DBMS also made possible a new syntax, the **Structured Query Language** (**SQL**), that allows information in an RDBMS to be accessed in all possible combinations.

**Relational database
model**

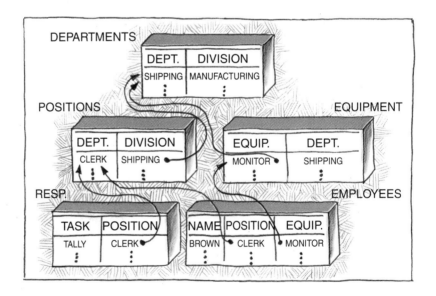

Although the relational model is much more flexible than its predecessors, it extracts a steep price for this flexibility. The information about complex relationships that was removed from the database must be expressed as procedures in every program that accesses the database, a clear violation of the independence required for software modularity. The shift from navigational to associative access also extracts a serious performance penalty for complex data because it takes much longer to locate related information by searching for content rather than jumping to calculated addresses. Comparisons have shown that it often takes 100 to 1,000 times longer to retrieve complex data structures from relational databases than it does from network databases.

Removing structure carries its own costs

Despite these drawbacks, the flexibility of relational databases has won over the industry. Although vast quantities of data continue to be managed in network databases, hierarchic databases, and unstructured files, these are the legacy of previous generations rather than reflections of current practice. Relational databases represent the dominant DBMS technology today, and virtually all new applications are constructed using relational systems.

Relational databases dominate today

Information Integration Through Data Warehousing

Data warehousing is now in vogue

Of course, having data scattered across several generations of DBMS technology presents its own set of problems. It is very hard for individual applications to integrate data across such radically different technologies, which means that getting any kind of management overview is still as hard as ever. The current approach to solving this problem is the **data warehouse**, a relational database that is used to pull together selected data from many different storage locations into a single repository with a common access mechanism. Data warehousing does not, in itself, solve the problem of integrating data from divergent sources. But it does allow that problem to be solved only once, using custom procedures to pull the data together. Once this has been done, all the combined data can be accessed in a uniform manner, using SQL and other standard tools.

A data warehouse

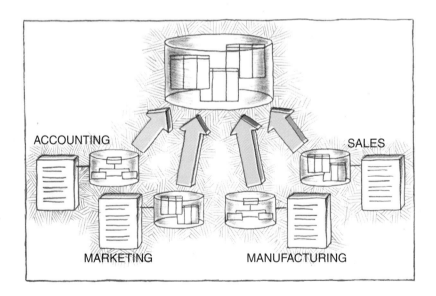

Data warehousing is a reasonable step toward data integration, but it's a solution that introduces problems of its own that are now becoming painfully apparent. One problem is that the rigidity of the data system is increased because any change to a local database requires changing the warehousing system. Another concern is the matter of timeliness. The information in the warehouse always lags behind the real-time operating data of the company, and the lag may differ when different databases are updated at different times. The result is that the management view of a company is always out of date to some degree and may be temporally inconsistent as well. Finally, there is the problem of scale. Data warehouses tend to exhibit uncontrolled growth, and attempts to manage this growth using tiers of warehouses only adds to the complexity and rigidity of the resulting system.

Data warehousing creates new problems

Suggested Readings

Object Technology

The first book is a general introduction to building enterprise-level systems using object technology. Cox's book remains a seminal introduction to the field, and it is the source of the analogy with the Industrial Revolution. Graham's book provides a high-level overview of the various methodologies available for analyzing, designing, and constructing systems with objects. The book by Orfali, Harkey, and Edwards offers a highly graphical and readable introduction to the complexities of object distribution. The book by Firesmith and Eykholt does the industry a great service by providing an extremely thorough and balanced guide to all the important terms and concepts of object technology.

Taylor, David. *Object-Oriented Information Systems: Planning and Implementation.* New York: Wiley, 1992.

Cox, Brad. *Object-Oriented Programming: An Evolutionary Approach.* Reading, Mass.: Addison-Wesley, 1986.

Graham, Ian. *Object-Oriented Methods.* Workingham, England: Addison-Wesley, 1991.

Orfali, Robert, Dan Harkey, and Jeri Edwards. *The Essential Distributed Objects Survival Guide.* New York: Wiley, 1996.

Firesmith, Donald, and Edward Eykholt. *Dictionary of Object Technology: The Definitive Desk Reference.* New York: SIGS Books, 1995.

Tools and Techniques

Coad and Mayfield's book offers a solid introduction to Java set in the context of good design practice, with a particularly insightful treatment of message interfaces. Cattell's book provides a thorough tour of object and extended relational databases but is not light reading. The book by Lorenz and Kidd offers a concise set of metrics to help analyze and optimize an object design. The design patterns book provides a collection of carefully crafted patterns that can be implemented with objects and used in a wide variety of situations. Fowler's book builds on this work and offers a set of patterns specifically designed for modeling common business situations.

Coad, Peter, and Mark Mayfield. *Java Design: Building Better Apps and Applets.* Upper Saddle River, N.J.: Prentice-Hall, 1997.

Cattell, Richard. *Object Data Management: Object-Oriented and Extended Relational Database Systems.* Reading, Mass.: Addison-Wesley, 1991.

Lorenz, Mark, and J. Kidd. *Object-Oriented Software Metrics.* Englewood Cliffs, N.J.: Prentice-Hall, 1994.

Gamma, Erich, Richard Helm, Ralph Johnson, and John Vlissides. *Design Patterns: Elements of Reusable Object-Oriented Software.* Reading, Mass.: Addison-Wesley, 1995.

Fowler, Martin. *Analysis Patterns: Reusable Object Models.* Reading, Mass.: Addison-Wesley, 1997.

Experiences and Guidelines

The first two books summarize the experiences of some of the top practitioners in the field and offer concrete guidelines for helping make object projects successful. Harmon and Morrissey's book provides an informative, well-packaged collection of case studies to learn from. Webster's book is a gem because it addresses many of the things that can go wrong with object technology and helps you avoid the pitfalls.

Goldberg, Adele, and Kenneth S. Rubin. *Succeeding with Objects: Decision Frameworks for Project Management.* Reading, Mass.: Addison Wesley Longman, 1995.

Love, Tom. *Object Lessons: Lessons Learned in Object-Oriented Development Projects.* New York: SIGS Books, 1993.

Harmon, Paul, and William Morrissey. *The Object Technology Casebook: Lessons from Award-Winning Business Applications.* New York: Wiley, 1996.

Webster, Bruce. *Pitfalls of Object-Oriented Development.* New York: Holt, 1995.

Business Engineering

These books all offer good insights into how objects can be used to improve business processes and structures. My own book is a brief overview in the spirit and format of the present book. The book by Khoshafian et al. is a comprehensive treatment of how objects can be used to transform organizations. The third book extends Ivar Jacobson's use-case methodology to address larger-scale business problems.

Taylor, David. *Business Engineering with Object Technology.* New York: Wiley, 1995.

Khoshafian, Setrag, Brad Baker, Razmik Abnous, and Kevin Shepherd. *Intelligent Offices: Object-Oriented Multi-Media Information Management in Client/Server Architectures.* New York: Wiley, 1992.

Jacobson, Ivar, Maria Ericsson, and Agneta Jacobson. *The Object Advantage: Business Process Reengineering with Object Technology.* Workingham, England: Addison-Wesley, 1995.

Complex Adaptive Systems

Kelly's book is not only a solid introduction to adaptive systems but also a great read that overflows with insights into how profoundly our world is changing. John Holland is one of the pioneers of the field, and his book is the next step for a deeper understanding of adaptive systems. Kauffman's book is the definitive work in the field, but it's not an easy read. Resnick's book is for those who want to play with adaptive systems and see them in action, either through his computer simulations or by downloading his software. Miller's book predates the formation of the field as a branch of science, but it offers one of the most comprehensive treatments of adaptive systems ever written.

Kelly, Kevin. *Out of Control: The New Biology of Machines, Social Systems, and the Economic World.* Reading, Mass.: Addison-Wesley, 1994.

Holland, John. *Hidden Order: How Adaptation Builds Complexity.* Reading, Mass.: Addison-Wesley, 1995.

Kauffman, Stuart A. *The Origins of Order: Self-Organization and Selection in Evolution.* New York: Oxford University Press, 1993.

Resnick, Mitchel. *Turtles, Termites, and Traffic Jams: Explorations in Massively Parallel Microworlds.* Cambridge, Mass.: MIT Press, 1997.

Miller, James Grier. *Living Systems.* New York: McGraw-Hill, 1978.

Organizations as Systems

Although these books do not reference object technology, systems theory, or research on complex adaptive systems, read them in the context of those topics and you will gain many valuable insights. Heirs and Pehrson's book is an absolute gem, providing a succinct analysis of how groups of people think and where collective thinking can exceed that of an individual. Zuboff's book is a comprehensive study of the effects of using technology to combine the knowledge of individuals, and Quinn's book has some excellent sections on this same topic. Schrage's work explores the tools as well as the effects of linking minds in an organization.

Heirs, Ben and Gordon Pehrson. *The Mind of the Organization.* New York: Harper & Row, 1982.

Zuboff, Soshana. *In the Age of the Smart Machine: The Future of Work and Power.* New York: Basic Books, 1988.

Quinn, James Brian. *Intelligent Enterprise: A Knowledge and Service Based Paradigm for Industry.* New York: Macmillan, 1992.

Schrage, Michael. *Shared Minds: New Technologies of Collaboration.* New York: Random House, 1990.

Glossary

4GL

An acronym for a fourth-generation language.

Abstract class

A class with no instances that is created only for the purpose of organizing a class hierarchy by defining methods and variables that will apply to lower-level classes.

API

An acronym for an application programming interface.

Application programming interface (API)

A software implementation technique that allows one program to control another program by invoking its procedures directly. More specifically, an API is a collection of procedures that a program makes available to other programs.

Associative access

The technique of using content, such as a name or a value, to locate records in a database. This technique is the major alternative to navigational access and is used primarily in relational DBMSs.

Binary large object (BLOB)

A set of binary information that is stored in a file and referenced by a DBMS. BLOBs are typically used to hold pictures, diagrams, and other information that is not readily managed by relational and other conventional database systems.

BLOB

An acronym for a binary large object.

C++

An object programming language developed at AT&T Bell Laboratories during the early 1980s. C++ is a "hybrid" language whose object features were grafted onto an existing language (C).

CASE

An acronym for computer-aided software engineering.

Class

A template for defining the methods and variables for a particular type of object. All objects of a given class are identical in form and behavior but contain different data in their variables.

Class hierarchy

A tree structure representing the inheritance relationships among a set of classes. A class hierarchy has a single top node (which may be the *Object* class) and may have any number of levels with any number of classes at each level.

Class library

A set of classes that have been designed to work together and are sold and installed as a package.

Collection class

A class that is designed to hold a variable number of references to other objects. Depending on the language, the terms *array* or *vector* may be used to designate classes with equivalent functionality.

COM

An acronym for the Component Object Model.

Common Object Request Broker Architecture (CORBA)

A specification for the ORB remote messaging services developed and promulgated by the Object Management Group (OMG).

Complex adaptive systems

Systems composed of relatively simple elements whose interactions allow them to exhibit higher levels of order and complexity than the elements themselves and to continuously modify the behavior of the system in response to environmental pressures.

Component Object Model (COM)

A technology developed by Microsoft to support pluggable objects. The technology implements most of the mechanisms of object technology but lacks support for inheritance.

Composite object

An object that contains one or more other objects, typically by storing references to those objects in its instance variables.

Computer-aided software engineering (CASE)

A collection of software tools that automate or support the process of designing and programming software systems.

CORBA

An acronym for the OMG's Common Object Request Broker Architecture. The acronym is trademarked by the OMG.

Data type

A generic description of an elementary unit of information in a particular software system. Common data types include whole numbers, decimal number, dollar amounts, dates, characters, and strings of characters.

Data warehouse

One or more databases used to aggregate data from operational databases for subsequent analysis of business processes. Data warehouses typically use relational DBMSs.

Database management system (DBMS)

A program that maintains and controls access to collections of related information in electronic files. Database managers provide many services, such as regulating simultaneous access by multiple users, restricting access to authorized people, and protecting the data against damage or accidental loss.

DBMS

An acronym for a database management system.

DCOM

An acronym for the Distributed Component Object Model.

Delegation

A design technique whereby an object passes a request for a service on to another object rather than handling the request itself. For example, a *Product* delegates the computation of volume discounts to a *Pricing* object that contains specialized methods and variables for computing these discounts.

Distributed Component Object Model (DCOM)

An extension of the COM architecture to support distributed objects. DCOM provides the communication services of an ORB but differs in many ways from CORBA, the ORB defined by the Object Management Group.

Dynamic load balancing

The ability to move computing operations among machines dynamically in order to make better use of the total available computing capacity.

Encapsulation

A technique in which data is packaged together with its corresponding procedures. In object technology, the mechanism for encapsulation is the object.

Extended relational DBMS

A relational DBMS with added functionality to handle the demands of storing and managing objects.

Fourth-generation language (4GL)

A type of computer language that accepts system requirements as input and generates a program to meet those requirements as output. Fourth-generation languages are useful primarily for well-understood procedures such as the generation of menus, forms, and reports.

Functional decomposition

A technique for analyzing a set of requirements and designing a program to meet those requirements. An overall goal for the program is broken down into a series of steps to meet that goal. Each step is then decomposed into more elementary steps, and so on. Each of the resulting components is programmed as a separate module.

Global data

Variables that are made available to all the procedures of a program, including the main routine and all of its subroutines. Global data is generally regarded as a serious violation of encapsulation because any change in the definition of global data can wreak havoc throughout a program.

Hierarchic model

A scheme for defining databases in which data elements are organized into hierarchical structures. The hierarchic model was developed in the 1960s and was the dominant type of database until the advent of the network model a decade later.

IDL

An acronym for the Interface Definition Language specified by the OMG.

IIOP

An acronym for the Internet Interoperability ORB Protocol promulgated by the OMG.

Information hiding

The technique of making the internal details of a module inaccessible to other modules, protecting the module from outside interference, and protecting other modules from relying on details that might change over time.

Inheritance

A mechanism whereby classes can make use of the methods and variables defined in all classes above them on their branch of the class hierarchy.

Instance

A term used to refer to an object that belongs to a particular class. For example, *California* is an instance of the class *State*. In some languages, instances are called the *members* of a class.

Interface

A generic term that refers to any communications surface that determines the signals that can pass through the surface. The term is used in this book and in the Java language as a shorthand reference to a message interface.

Interface Definition Language (IDL)

A specification promulgated by the OMG for defining message interfaces for remote communications over an ORB. The term is trademarked by the OMG.

Internet

A global communication network that uses telephone lines and other media to allow users to send messages and other information to one another.

Internet Interoperability ORB Protocol (IIOP)

A communications protocol developed by the OMG to extend the capabilities of CORBA-based ORBs. The protocol allows ORBs created by different vendors to interoperate, and it supports the use of the Internet as its communication medium.

Java

A relatively new object language developed by Sun Microsystems. Java is based on the syntax of C and combines some of the best features of C++ and Smalltalk. It is platform-independent, supports mobile objects, and is specifically adapted for execution over the Internet.

Keyboard emulator

A software tool that mimics the output of an end user terminal connected to a mainframe or other host computer. A keyboard emulator allows programs to simulate a user typing commands at a keyboard in order to control programs that lack APIs. It is generally used in connection with screen scraper technologies.

Legacy system

An existing software system that is currently executing business operations and must be taken into consideration when designing new systems.

Location transparency

The ability to mask the location of an object so that other objects can send messages to it without having to route those messages to a particular machine.

Message

A signal from one object to another that requests the receiving object to carry out one of its methods. A message consists of three parts: the name of the receiver, the method it is to carry out, and any parameters the method may require to fulfill its charge.

Message interface

A set of signatures that determines what messages an object can respond to. A message interface can include other message interfaces, allowing interfaces to be mixed and matched across objects.

Message signature

A specification of the form and composition of a particular message. Although definitions vary, a message signature is usually viewed as specifying the name of the message and one or more parameters that must be given values when the message is sent.

Method

A procedure defined within a class.

Modular programming

A general approach to programming in which programs are broken down into components, or *modules*, each of which contains its own procedures and data. The central tenet of modular programming is that modules should be as independent as possible from one another, with interactions being minimized and tightly controlled.

Navigational access

The technique of using location-based references, such as storage addresses or offsets, to locate records in a database. This technique is the primary alternative to associative access and is used in network, hierarchic, and object DBMSs.

Network model

A scheme for defining databases in which data elements may be interconnected to any degree, forming arbitrarily complex structures. The network model was developed in the 1970s to overcome the structural limitations of the earlier hierarchic model.

Object

A software packet containing a collection of related methods and data. The term is used inconsistently in the literature, referring sometimes to instances and other times to classes. In this book, the term *object* refers to a specific instance of a class but includes the characteristics of that class. Thus, an object may be said to contain methods even though its methods are actually defined in its class.

Object database management system (ODBMS)

A database management system built specifically to store and retrieve objects rather than simple data types.

Object engine

A multiuser object environment that provides both persistence and execution. These tools are often classified with object DBMSs but differ from these more conventional database products in that they support method execution within the DBMS.

Object Management Group (OMG)

An industry group dedicated to promoting object technology and fostering the standardization of that technology. The OMG is sponsored by more than 700 organizations who either market or use object-oriented products.

Object request broker (ORB)

A communications protocol for conveying messages between objects. ORBs are usually used for communications between objects located on different machines. The protocol is language-independent, allowing objects written in different programming languages to interact with one another.

Object technology

A set of principles guiding software construction together with languages, databases, and other tools that support those principles. The defining principles are encapsulation, polymorphism, and inheritance. In this book, the term is synonymous with the term *object-oriented technology* and is preferred because it is shorter and simpler.

ODBMS

An acronym for an object database management system.

OMG

An acronym for the Object Management Group.

ORB

An acronym for an object request broker.

OSQL

An acronym for an object-oriented variant of SQL, the Structured Query Language used to retrieve information from relational databases.

Overriding

A special case of polymorphism in which the same name is given to a method or variable at two or more levels on the same branch of a class hierarchy. When this happens, the name that is lowest in the hierarchy takes precedence, overriding the more generic definitions further up the hierarchy.

Paradigm

An acquired way of thinking about something that shapes thought and action in ways that are both conscious and unconscious. Paradigms are essential because they provide a culturally shared model for how to think and act, but they can present major obstacles to adopting newer and better approaches.

Paradigm shift

A transition from one paradigm to another. Paradigm shifts typically meet with considerable resistance followed by gradual acceptance as the superiority of the new paradigm becomes apparent. Object technology is regarded by many people as a paradigm shift in software development.

Parameter

An object or a data element that is included in a message to provide the requested method with information it needs to perform its task. A message may include any number of parameters, including zero.

Persistent object

An object that must maintain its existence and its internal values from one run of a program to the next. Persistent objects may be stored in files or databases.

Polymorphism

The ability to hide different implementations behind a common interface, simplifying the communications among objects. For example, defining a unique *print* method for each kind of document in a system would allow any document to be printed by sending the message *print,* without concern for how that method was actually carried out for a given document.

Procedure

A sequence of instructions to a computer indicating how a particular task should be carried out.

Proxy object

An object that represents another object located on a remote machine. The proxy object accepts messages on behalf of the real object and forwards these messages to that object. Proxy objects are used to achieve location and remoteness transparency.

Receiver

The object to which a message is sent. A sender object passes a message to the receiver object, which processes the message and then passes back a return value.

Record

A generic term for a data entry in an information management system. As used in this book, it is a member of one of the structures defined by a DBMS. Example: a row in a table defined by a relational DBMS.

Relational model

A scheme for defining databases in which data elements are organized into relations, typically viewed as rows in tables. The relational model was developed in the 1980s to provide a more flexible alternative to the hierarchic and network models, which could not be easily restructured.

Remote Method Invocation (RMI)

A technique used by Java programs to manage communications among remote objects. It provides the basic functionality of an ORB but does not offer the same feature set as CORBA.

Remoteness transparency

The ability to hide the fact that an object may be located on a different machine, allowing local objects to send messages to it as though it were in the same execution space.

Return value

An object or a data type that a receiver object passes to a sender object in response to a message.

RMI

An acronym for Java's Remote Method Invocation mechanism.

Runtime library

A set of software procedures stored in executable form that may be invoked from an executing program.

Screen scraper

A software technology for reading text flowing onto an end user terminal connected to a mainframe or other host computer. A screen scraper allows programs to access information from other programs that lack APIs. It is generally used in conjunction with a keyboard emulation tool.

Sender

The object initiating a message. A sender object passes a message to a receiver object and then waits for it to pass back a return value.

Signature

As used in this book, a shorthand reference to a message signature.

Simula

A computer language developed in the 1960s at the Norwegian Computer Center for the purpose of simulating real-world processes. Simula pioneered the concepts of classes, objects, and messages, and it provided object-based support for parallel processing.

Smalltalk

An object programming language developed at Xerox PARC (Palo Alto Research Center) in the early 1970s.

Source code control system

A software system for managing the sequences of instructions, or *source code*, that programmers type into a computer when they are writing software. Source code control systems maintain copies of the source code and track successive versions as the source code is changed.

SQL

An acronym for the Structured Query Language.

Structured programming

A collection of techniques designed to increase the rigor of software development and to improve the quality of development systems. Modular programming and functional decomposition are central to structured programming.

Structured Query Language (SQL)

A standardized syntax for requesting information from relational DBMSs and performing operations on these systems.

Subclass

A class that is a special case of another class. For example, *Fox* is a special case of *Mammal.*

Subroutine

A sequence of instructions that has been defined as a separate unit within a program, allowing the unit to be invoked anywhere in the program simply by including its name as one of the instructions.

Superclass

A class that is higher in the class hierarchy than another class. For example, *Mammal* is a superclass of *Fox.* In some languages, a superclass is referred to as a *base class*. The terms *parent class* and *ancestor class* may be used to refer to the immediate superclass or to all classes above a given class in the hierarchy, respectively.

Variable

A named storage place within an object for a data element. The data element can be a built-in data type, such as a number or a character, or it can be a reference to another object.

Wrapping

As used in this book, placing an object interface around nonobject software in order to allow that software to be accessed by an object system. The programming code that implements the interface is often called a *wrapper*. The technique is also known as *wrappering*.

Index

Object Solutions

Managing the Object-Oriented Project
Grady Booch
Addison-Wesley Object Technology Series

Object Solutions is a direct outgrowth of Grady Booch's experience with object-oriented projects in development around the world. This book focuses on the development process and is the perfect resource for developers and managers who want to implement object technologies for the first time or refine their existing object-oriented development practice. The book is divided into two major sections. The first four chapters describe in detail the process of object-oriented development in terms of inputs, outputs, products, activities, and milestones. The remaining ten chapters provide practical advice on key issues including management, planning, reuse, and quality assurance. Drawing upon his knowledge of strategies used in both successful and unsuccessful projects, Grady Booch offers pragmatic advice for applying object technologies and controlling projects effectively.

0-8053-0594-7 • Paperback • 336 pages • 1996
http://www.aw.com/cseng/books/0-8053-0594-7/

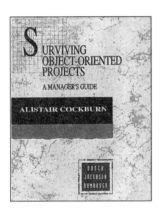

Surviving Object-Oriented Projects

A Manager's Guide
Alistair Cockburn

The survival and ultimate success of an object-oriented software development project hinges on the project manager's prior planning and knowledge of what to expect, and their active management to keep the project on track. This book provides managers with numerous heuristics that are designed to enable managers to solve and avoid the most common problems found in object-oriented projects. The book addresses issues of scheduling, budgeting, staffing, and cost-justification—all supported and illustrated by short case studies of actual projects. The final chapter collects these heuristics into brief lists for quick reference.

0-201-49834-0 • Paperback • 272 pages • 1998 • Available Fall 1997
http://www.aw.com/cseng/books/0-201-49834-0/

Software Reuse

Architecture, Process and Organization for Business Success
Ivar Jacobson, Martin Griss, and Patrik Jonsson
Addison-Wesley Object Technology Series

This long-awaited book brings software engineers, designers, programmers, and their managers a giant step closer to a future in which object-oriented component-based software engineering is the norm. Jacobson, Griss, and Jonsson develop a coherent model and set of guidelines for ensuring success with large-scale, systematic, OO reuse. Their framework, referred to as "Reuse-Driven Software Engineering Business" (Reuse Business) deals systematically with the key business process, architecture, and organization issues that hinder success with reuse.

0-201-92476-5 • Hardcover • 512 pages • 1997
http://www.aw.com/cseng/books/0-201-92476-5/

The Mythical Man Month
Essays on Software Engineering, Anniversary Edition
Frederick P. Brooks, Jr.

No book on software project management has been as influential and timeless as *The Mythical Man-Month*. Blending software engineering facts with thought-provoking opinions, Fred Brooks offers insight into managing the development of complex computer systems. In this twentieth anniversary edition, the original text is accompanied by the author's current advice and thoughts based on the newest developments in the computer industry. In four added chapters, including his 1986 article "No Silver Bullet," Brooks asks whether there is yet a silver bullet for software productivity and gives his latest opinions on the mythical man-month.

0-201-83595-9 • Paperback • 336 pages • 1995
http://www.aw.com/cseng/books/0-201-83595-9/

Managing Technical People
Innovation, Teamwork, and the Software Process
Watts S. Humphrey

In previous books, Humphrey established "process" as a key factor in successful software development. Now he focuses on the critical role of innovative people and gives concrete advice on how to identify, motivate, and organize these people into highly productive teams. Drawing on extensive experience as a senior manager of software development at IBM, Humphrey presents proven leadership practices and management techniques. Learn from the master the specific steps you can take to encourage greater innovation while attaining higher levels of efficiency and quality.

0-201-54597-7 • Paperback • 352 pages • 1997
http://www.aw.com/cseng/books/0-201-54597-7/

Introduction to the Personal Software Process℠
Watts S. Humphrey
SEI Series in Software Engineering

One of the major challenges software engineers face transcends designing and programming software applications: it is managing their own personal approach to the software engineering process—to overcome the "hacker" ethic and work more effectively, efficiently, and productively. This hands-on book provides practical exercises you can use to improve your time management and quality assurance practices—exercises that develop skills to help you do competent, professional work and better apply your programming expertise. This is a must-have book for serious software developers who want to elevate their work habits and personal software management techniques.

0-201-54809-7 • Paperback • 304 pages • 1997
http://www.aw.com/cseng/books/0-201-54809-7/

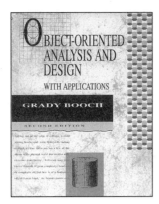

Object-Oriented Analysis and Design, Second Edition
With Applications
Grady Booch
Addison-Wesley Object Technology Series

While the first edition of this book was instrumental in making object-oriented technology a practical reality, the second edition draws upon the rich and varied results of hundreds of projects to offer improved methods for object development and a new unified notation. With many examples, all implemented in C++, Booch illustrates essential concepts, explains the method, and shows successful applications including a client-server architecture and an application framework. You will also find pragmatic advice on key issues including classification, implementation strategies, and cost-effective project management.

0-8053-5340-2 • Hardcover • 608 pages • 1994
http://www.aw.com/cseng/books/0-8053-5340-2/

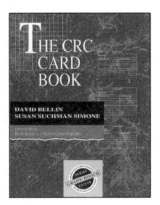

The CRC Card Book
David Bellin and Susan Suchman Simone
Forewords by Kent Beck and Ward Cunningham
Addison-Wesley Object Technology Series

CRC cards help project teams "act out" the various parts of a problem domain. The application developer can use these cards to define the Classes, the Relationships between classes, and the Collaboration between these classes (CRC) prior to beginning the OO design of the application program. The case studies in this book are presented in the engaging style of a novella to demonstrate how personalities and organizational culture come into play when using the CRC technique. C++, Java, and Smalltalk experts provide implementation examples in each language. This book demonstrates how to discover classes through team brainstorming, manage an object-oriented project, refine project requirements, test the conception of the system, and evaluate potential paths of collaboration using role play.

0-201-89535-8 • Paperback • 320 pages • 1997
http://www.aw.com/cseng/books/0-201-89535-8/

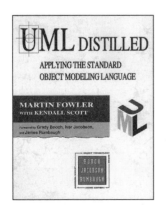

UML Distilled
Applying the Standard Object Modeling Language
Martin Fowler with Kendall Scott
Addison-Wesley Object Technology Series

This book introduces the Unified Modeling Language—sure to become the new standard in object technology. It focuses on the core UML notation that users will need to know, and presents UML in the context of real world software development, not as an isolated notation. *UML Distilled* represents the first published look at the Objectory Software Development Process, the merging of OMT, Booch, and OOSE. The book also discusses important techniques that are not part of UML but are key to successful object-oriented development, such as CRC Cards, Patterns, and Refactoring.

0-201-32563-2 • Paperback • 208 pages • 1997
http://www.aw.com/cseng/books/0-201-32563-2/